Eyes of the Beholders

Life Stories of African American Women

Amy

Thank you for your support

Deris Thomas

678-422-4975

www.wisemenusa.com

Edited by Eric Brown

Library of Congress Control Number: 2022937476
ISBN: 978-1-7334656-7-0 (pbk.)

Published by Sumner House Publishing
a Division of Wisemen Multimedia, LLC
Atlanta, Georgia, USA
www.sumnerhousepublishing.com

Printed in the United States of America

DEDICATION

This anthology is dedicated in loving memory to
a distinguished woman who worked tirelessly for Sumner
House but did not make it with us to the end.

Connie Lerner

1961 - 2020

Thank you for your contributions.

FOREWORD

The Golden Writers recognizes that each member of our
group is unique. We grew up in different geographical
areas and home environments. Our experiences are not
the same. We are unique people who accept that diversity
can highlight differences and similarities. Having
acknowledged our differences, we have come together as a
group.

Our life events have brought us to our current state of
being and will heavily influence our futures. Our view of
the world around us has been shaped by our experiences.
We aspire to use the lessons that our various backgrounds
have to offer to help others in similar situations. We hope
that our stories will give our great-great-great
grandchildren a glimpse into our lives. Maybe they too will
be guided by what we have written. Perhaps stories of past
events in our lives will let them know that we understand
their condition, situation, or struggle.

Our empathy comes from similar experiences. Maybe our
stories are worth telling because they get a chuckle or make
someone smile. These are some of the reasons we have
written this collection of short memoirs. These are our
stories and we have told them in a manner that we want
our stories to be told.

It is with this intention that we, the Golden Writers, started
on our memoirs. In some cases, we have chosen to enhance
our stories with pictures. Please note these are not
attempts to give complete chronological events of our lives.
These writings are not meant to be autobiographies. These
are simply some of the life experiences we can never forget.

ACKNOWLEDGEMENTS

Clayton County Senior Centers have always felt like country clubs to us. It is at one of these centers that the Golden Writers were born.

Regardless of our individual paths, our lives have been enriched by the interactive, creative process of discovering the inner writer in all of us.

We would like to thank the staff of the Griswell Senior Center for their time and generosity.

Many thanks go out to all who helped to make this publication possible.

TABLE OF CONTENTS

"My mission in life is not merely to survive, but to thrive; and to do so with some passion, some compassion, some humor, and some style."

Maya Angelou —

American poet, memoirist, and civil rights activist

WHY AFRICAN AMERICAN WOMEN OVER 55 SHOULD WRITE THEIR STORIES

by Doris Thomas

In my humble opinion, it would be hard pressed to find any other race of women who have given as much, love as much, or allowed themselves to be neglected as much as the African American woman. It is so important to write your own stories. Writing stories can bring revelation, knowledge, understanding, and peace to your spirit, soul, and body—not to mention helping others who have had the same experiences but thought they were alone.

We owe it to ourselves and those coming behind us and walking in this present day to tell our stories so they may be passed on—to leave our footprint in the sand, showing that we have made a difference no matter how large or small. We need to tell our stories to help others, older and younger, understand that writing purges the ghosts of the past, present, and future. We can show how we have overcome and/or may still be dealing with experiences that could have destroyed us, crippled us, made us lose our minds, yet we stand.

Those who are continuing to right the wrongs done to them, those who are excavating the trash and garbage dumped on them—many not even aware it was being dumped and many because they thought they were helping others by allowing the trash and garbage to be dumped on them—can all benefit from writing.

It is important for us as African American women to share our stories to inspire other African American women to tell their stories—even when others may not want them

9

to because of what it might say about them. But remember, it's your story, not theirs.

God made us for a purpose—no matter our age. If we don't know our purpose, have not been living it, or are afraid to find it and live it out loud, then it's time. Own it. Be it. If you do, then I bet it will change your life, invigorate you, and change your perspective on all things great or small. May you be strengthened as you go forth in writing your stories inspiring others because God is the Power that is within you.

After I wrote this, I had to have a procedure called a myelogram, which requires an area of the body to be numbed and injected with contrast. The patient has to take different positions, so the doctor can follow the contrast as it moves through the spaces in the spine. These positions can be very uncomfortable. The doctor conducting my procedure asked me if I would mind if he and the technologist talked while he worked. He said that the technologist liked to tell stories though he felt she probably was lying, and in response, she told him the devil is a lie. I didn't mind hearing her stories because I figured it would help keep my mind off the procedure. I also told them I was taking a class called *Write Your Story* at the Senior Citizen Center I attend.

Interestingly, the doctor asked if I would share one of my stories, so I shared a little of the *Moonshine* story. The doctor was impressed and told me I should continue to write my stories, noting that my grandchildren will appreciate it. He said he wished his grandparents had written stories like that for him. Although this doctor was white, I think it was a good example of why it's so important to write our stories down. The doctor had never heard of the poison liquor story and found it very interesting. So, as I said earlier, write your story and leave your footprints on the world.

LOVE AND KISSES – oooXXXoooXXX

by Penny Duncan Stephens

Many years ago, an unexpected, dreadful chain of events occurred, and a family unit of six—a father, mother, and four children—became what I imagine any good family fears most: divided.

When I was two years old, a truant officer came to our house to find out why my sister and brother had missed so many days of school. He quickly discovered my eight-year-old sister had been caring for three siblings—my six-year-old brother, five-year-old sister, and me—by herself. There was no adult supervision in our home until the evening when my father came home. That was all it took for the truant officer to begin the process of removing us from our home and placing us in foster care.

My father worked long hours in construction to keep us fed and support his drinking habit. My mom had a series of nervous breakdowns. She was diagnosed with schizophrenia and had been admitted to Eloise, a mental hospital not too far from where we lived.

When my father realized that the state was going to take us away, he scooped me up—just me—with a few belongings and took me to live with Mr. and Mrs. Smith. They were an older couple in the neighborhood, recommended to my father by a friend, who believed they would take care of me until he could do better. Later, I found out that he purposely took me, and not the other children, because I was so young, and he thought someone may adopt me. He feared he would never see me again. Since my siblings were older, he believed there was less chance of them being adopted. In hindsight, there was some truth to his madness, because somehow, he was always able to find my brother and sisters in different foster homes and bring us all together to go visit my mother from time to time.

I was born Penny Maude Burton. Yes, that was my actual birth name, not Penny for my first name or Maude for my middle name—straight out, altogether, "Pennymaude." I still laugh out loud when I say the name. I'm sure Mrs. Smith had a laugh or two before she shared that tidbit of information with me. Thankfully when the Smiths adopted me at age five, they legally named me Penny Ann Smith, which I believe suits me better.

I often wonder at such a young age how I could remember the day my father left me with the Smiths. He told me he would come back for me in about a week or so. I remember crying as he left. Unfortunately, that week turned into years. Up until about the time I was ready to start kindergarten, I had not seen or heard from either of my parents. But I remember one day being taken to a courthouse. Inside, a lady took me by the hand and told me she had someone she wanted me to meet. We walked together to a room that I remember had the tallest, most massive wooden doors I had ever seen. The lady told me to go inside and walk down the aisle. I replied, "I don't see anyone," but then a person peered out from one of the wooden benches. I recognized her. It was my mother, and she was crying. She sat me on her lap and tearfully explained that she had to sign papers to give me up for adoption because she had been hospitalized and could not care for me anymore.

My permanent address was 29005 Northlawn, Detroit, Michigan until I turned 15 years of age. My time with the Smiths was traumatic to say the least. Mrs. Smith was very mean to me. In that household, I was mentally and physically abused. I believe she did the best she knew how with me, but it was not a healthy environment for a young girl. Now, I realize I was trapped in a rigid, Southern upbringing at the hands of my adoptive parents. We lived in the North, but they were raised in the South by former slaves, a mentality that was still ingrained in their minds and spirits.

Penny Duncan Stephens

My adopted parents were very strict. I rarely had the opportunity to go anywhere to have fun, but I was allowed to be around family outside our home. The Smiths had a 30-year-old grandson, who was married with three children. I would spend the weekend with them from time-to-time. I enjoyed being there because I had a great time with the kids. The woman of the house, his wife, worked the night shift, so it was just me, the husband, and the kids in the house after dark. One day, the husband asked me if I wanted to watch a late-night movie on TV with him. I remember being around 10 years old on this particular occasion. I immediately felt special and said *yes*. Under normal circumstances, he never let me stay up past nine, but that time was the exception, and I was so excited. He told me to go ahead and go to bed with the kids like usual, and he would come and get me after the kids were asleep.

I did as agreed and went to bed with the kids. Later, he came to get me just like he'd promised. However, when we went back into the TV room, I noticed all the lights were out. The room was dimly lit by the glow of the television. It was suspicious, but we actually did watch a movie. Afterwards though, he guided me to his bedroom. With his wife working the nightshift, I found myself alone with him in their bedroom. At first, I didn't know why he'd brought me in there, but I soon found out. He pulled down my nightgown and told me to lay on the bed—I did. Then, he fondled me and pulled out a switchblade knife which he proudly waved around in front of my face. He threatened me that if I said anything to anyone about what he was doing to me that night, he would kill me.

My adoptive mother, Mrs. Smith, always told me that if anyone touched the hem of my dress, I would get pregnant. I didn't know what that meant but I knew what happened that night involved a lot more than the hem of my dress, which was not good. I was so afraid to say anything to anyone. Eventually, about a year later, I confided in my best girlfriend, and I told her that I thought I might be pregnant. I figured she would give me good advice, but in the back of my mind, I believed the grandson's threat was real. I felt like I was putting us both at risk, but I still needed some guidance.

My girlfriend asked me if I had missed my cycle, and I asked her what that was. Mrs. Smith never talked to me about much of anything important, and I was only able to answer *yes, ma'am* or *no, ma'am* to questions at home. Basically, I could not speak unless I was spoken to first. I was never allowed to be in the presence of adults when they were talking, so I had no clue what my girlfriend was talking about. But then she educated me, stating that had I gotten pregnant, I would have had the baby by now. "It only takes nine months to have a baby," she explained, "and you said this happened over a year ago, right?" I felt so stupid, but at the same time relieved that my fear of being pregnant was over. I confided in my girlfriend but asked her not to breathe a word to anyone.

I was about 12 years old when I got my cycle. When I finally told Mrs. Smith about the molestation, she told me not to tell anyone—especially not Mr. Smith. Then she told me to keep away from her grandson. Without skipping a beat, she went right into victim-blaming, suggesting it was probably something that I did to make the grandson do what he did to me.

Mrs. Smith constantly pelted me with unkind words. Her belittling made me feel helpless and unwanted. Mr. Smith allowed her to carry out the discipline while he remained silent. He was always a man of few words.

At age 15, I remember Mrs. Smith telling me that I could go and babysit her grandson's children. By then the grandson, like his wife, was working nights, which meant there would be no one home to take care of the children. I was shocked she asked me because of what had happened several years before, but I was taught not to question adults. The Smiths raised me to believe that no matter what an adult told me to do, I was to always obey. Despite the past incident, I was happy to get out of the house for the summer and make a little babysitting money as well.

One night, while sleeping on the couch, I was awakened by the stereo's volume. It was so loud. When I opened my eyes, I found the grandson on top of me, threatening me not to make a sound. That night's attack led to me missing my next menstrual cycle and before long the morning sickness came. I didn't need to seek advice at that time—I knew I was pregnant. I managed to tell my sister whose foster mom was a member of our church. Her mom told me that I needed to report what had happened—she explained it was incest. So, she took me to the police station, I filed a report, and the grandson was picked up. Yet he denied what had happened. The police then made him take a lie detector test, of which the results proved my story was true. My parents were called in, but they refused to press charges on their grandson, so he was released, and I had to go back to live with the Smiths.

Needless to say, the situation at home was unpleasant. My parents withdrew me from school and kept me at home where they called me terrible names and forced me to suffer through constant mental and physical abuse. Back when I was at the police station, a social worker had secretly given me her business card. She felt very sad that I had to return to the conditions I had been enduring. She told me to call her if I needed to talk. I called her numerous times, crying because of the abuse. Mrs. Smith said awful things to me about the sexual abuse. She blamed me, which made me feel abandoned for the second time in my life, and I was only 15. Aren't parents and guardians supposed to defend and protect their child? None of that was apparent to me. When she told me that it was all my fault, I just sank deeper into the feeling that I did not belong to anyone. It was as if someone had cut my heart in two. If I ever had any love for Mrs. Smith, it was lost. From that point, the woman I had called *mama* for 13 years would only be known to me as Mrs. Smith—with no attached feelings.

Almost every day was like a horrific nightmare at home, but we went to church every Sunday, my only saving grace. Being there gave me a good spiritual foundation. It was the only real thing I had to hang onto. I didn't realize it at the time, but I know now that God was working in the background with the social worker that I had shared my unhappiness with, and it was for the better.

One day, a policewoman came to our house with a petition to remove me from the home—no questions asked. She told me to get my things and said that she was taking me to a Salvation Army home for unwed mothers. I had such mixed emotions at that time. I truly wanted to go but I also felt very sad that I was leaving the only home I had known for the last 13 years of my life.

I remained at the Salvation Army facility for five months. I thought I would be going back to live with the Smiths after the baby was delivered. The plan was for me to give the baby up for adoption. I had already signed the documents, but then something unexpected happened.

After giving birth, I was assigned another social worker. She visited me in the hospital and asked me how I was feeling.

"Very sad," I answered.

She said, "How would you like to keep your baby?"

I told her that the Smiths would not allow me to bring my baby home.

The social worker said, "We have contacted your real mother, and she wants you and the baby to come live with her. She will watch the baby while you finish high school."

I felt as if God had opened up the gates of heaven and poured me out a blessing—too much to receive.

This was a true miracle, beyond my wildest dreams. Even though the papers had been signed for me to give my baby up for adoption, I was able to see my little girl, who I named Tina Marie. I took her to our new home to live with my real mother. On the second day with my mom, I received a package and card from my maternal grandmother, Maude, who lived in Hamilton, Ontario.

My mother told me I was named after my grandmother. I never had the opportunity to meet my grandmother face—to—face, but the greeting card she sent me was signed at the bottom with XXX's and OOO's. I thought it was some French jargon. I didn't have the slightest idea what it meant and did not ask anyone. I was so young, sheltered, and naive.

Penny Duncan Stephens and Tina Marie

After graduating from high school at the age of 17, I was so proud to be a mom that I decided to go visit the Smiths, so they could meet Tina Marie—she was so cute. Sadly, Mr. Smith had suffered a stroke, and Mrs. Smith was in the late stages of dementia. They had no one to take care of them. Even though I had such bad experiences while living with them, there was no way I could leave them without any assistance. I helped them as much as I could, taking them to the doctor, church, grocery store, and I helped them with the cleaning and cooking. Ultimately, I helped them with selling their home and getting them in a nice nursing home until their later demise.

Later in life, I witnessed someone sign a greeting card they were sending, and they signed it just like my grandmother signed mine years before. They told me they always sign their cards with XXX's and OOO's, and that it meant "love and kisses." What a joy to find that profound meaning after all those years!

Love and Kisses to you too, grandmother. I will never forget your letters, and telephone calls that made me feel your arms of affection all the way from Canada. Your spirit still lives on in me.

Tina Marie (my daughter)

Over the years, I have been able to share my story with others and speak into the lives of young ladies to let them know that in the midst of adversity, they are not alone. Learning to love yourself doesn't mean it's your fault. If you have a similar story like this, don't give up, hang in there, my story of being an overcomer can be your story, too. Love and Kisses XXXOOOXXX's.

THE FIRE IN MY LIFE

by Penny Duncan Stephens

*In the last story, I talked about my early life,
my struggles, and my wonderful daughter
Tina Marie. Though it may seem that I
already told this loving story, there's still
more to tell—more wonder and awe about
that challenging, yet magical time in my life.
I endeavor to share the details of this time
and the depths of my joy in the following
story, The Fire in My Life.*

By the time I was 16 years old, my life was taking a turn for the best. Up until now, I felt as if I was trapped in a vacuum with no way out. Now, I know that no one can dictate your destiny. It is a divine journey that God has planned for you with crooks and turns. Fair? No. A lot of the time it does not feel that justice will play a fair hand in your life. Just hang around to see what your journey has in store for you. You will be amazed at how your life can make a complete turnaround.

The last few years of my childhood felt as if I had been trapped in this downward spiral of unhappy events— abandonment, lies, deceit, mental and physical abuse, secrets, guilt, shame, rape, and having to face the decision to give my unborn baby up for adoption. This decision was actually being made for me. I was in a home for unwed mothers in Detroit, Michigan, waiting to deliver a child who was the product of me being raped by the 30-year-old grandson of my adopted parents. The very person that had taken advantage of me lied and said he didn't do it. Not only had he raped me, but he also took the liberty of fondling me when I was only about 10 years of age. Fortunately, the results of his lie detector test were on my side—the side of the truth.

I didn't think there were any hopes of me standing up for myself and refusing to return to live with my adopted parents. I truly believed I had no choice. In my mind, all I could see was me at sixteen years old, returning to a life chock full of all the unhappiness no teenage girl should have to endure. I had nothing to look forward to, literally.

But one day, I received a visit from a lady who said she was my assigned social worker. I remember she came two days after I delivered my daughter. I was unable to see my baby or name her since I was forced to sign papers in advance to give her up for adoption. But, when the social worker came in, she asked me a question that changed my life forever—*would you like to keep your baby?* I imagine the expression on my face at that time was one of sheer confusion. I knew my adopted parents would not let me bring a baby home, and, of course, the adoption papers had already been signed.

This wonderful lady social worker dug into my background and found my real mother. Mom had been plagued by mental problems in the past. She had several nervous breakdowns and was diagnosed with schizophrenia. She had been institutionalized for a long time—a fate that separated her from her four children. My other three siblings were placed in foster homes, and I had been adopted.

Despite Mom's early challenges, the social worker discovered that Mom had more recently been leading a productive life with the aid of medicine to keep her depression and anxiety in check. Once we were reunited, my mother told me that she was sorry for our family being separated, and that she would try to make up for the years we had all lost. Mom proceeded to show me a love that I had never been shown before. The difference was night and day compared to my home life with my adoptive parents. I was so happy to finally feel what real love and the warm touch of someone who genuinely cares for me could be like. And it was more than just love for me. Mom doted over little miss Tina with a grandmother's love that I truly believe every child needs and deserves.

When Mom told me that I could live with her and finish high school while she cared for little Tina Marie, I couldn't believe what I was hearing—it was something like a fairytale. My thoughts of unhappiness that stemmed from the prospect of returning to my adoptive parents' home, quickly evolved into unbridled happiness. The chance to finally live with my real mother again and bring my newborn to my new home too was like heaven to me. I had not lived with my mom since I was two years old, and the word *overjoyed* hardly gave this wonderful opportunity justice.

After settling into my new high school, my school counselors directed me to take co-op classes which afforded me the opportunity to do classwork the first part of the day, and then go to work for four hours after school. This was very productive for me. I interviewed and was hired for my first real job as a cashier at a five and dime store called Kresge. This new chapter of my life was progressing well. I graduated from high school at age 17. I was so proud of my accomplishments because I had often been taunted with unkind words from my adoptive parents—they constantly told me that I would never amount to anything. Every chance they got, they proclaimed I would never finish school and be burdened with a bunch of babies, but they were wrong.

I was continuing to move upward in life. I applied to Kresge's Main Office and, at age 18, landed the perfect job in the import department. After passing the test for the position, I was then able to put the secretarial skills I gained in my last few years of high school to use—typing, shorthand, proofreading, and accounting. Can you imagine me at age 18—no longer having to stand on my feet seven or eight hours a day, working a cash register? At my new job, I had a nice big desk, a swivel desk chair, my own typewriter, and a salary of $310 a month. I had to pinch myself because it felt like I was dreaming. The Lord knew I was in Seventh Heaven.

The sheer perceived enormity of my accomplishment gave me a big boost in confidence and self-esteem. I rebounded in life, having survived being an unwanted, raped, embarrassed, pregnant teenager. I was finally coming into my own. Finally, I felt like I was worthy of all the good that life was beginning to afford me at my young age.

It was difficult sometimes to understand who I was or how to love myself. No one had ever told me that I needed to do that. However, I realized I needed to learn to love myself before I could really love others and the universe. My adopted mom, Mrs. Smith, religiously told me I was "never going to amount to anything" and that I "wasn't worth the salt in my bread." She had many other sayings that in hindsight I believe were the product of the slave mentality she had as a direct result of her upbringing. After hearing such negative proclamations day in and day out, my self-esteem suffered greatly. I remember feeling like I was never "enough" or that I never did anything right. I was always in hot water with my adopted mom.

Well, let's get on with this story....

About five months into my new job, my boss called me into his office and said I needed to take a call from the personnel department. I could not imagine what they were calling me for, but in my mind, I hoped it was not because I had done something wrong. When I got to the phone, the lady on the other end of the line told me to call a number right away. I did as I was instructed, and it turns out the number I dialed belonged to my neighbor from across the street. She was calling to tell me there was an emergency at my home. She said to get home as soon as possible. The way she behaved frightened me, so I immediately asked, "what's wrong?" but she wouldn't say. She just told me to get home as soon as possible, and they would explain when I got there.

Since I commuted by bus each day, I told her it might take me an hour or so to get home. People in that era got around mostly by bus unless you were fortunate enough to own a car. She instructed me to take a cab and she would pay for it if I did not have the money. That bumped my fear factor up even higher, but I still did what she told me.

As mentioned before, my mother was caring for my daughter who was now about two years old. Upon taking a cab home there were police cars and fire engines in front of my house. I was greeted by the neighbor who had called my place of employment.

We lived upstairs in a two-family flat and I was greeted by the neighbor. She said "Penny, I did not want to tell you over the phone because I didn't want to upset you. Early this morning I saw smoke coming from the windows of your house and called the fire department."

As she was telling me the story, I was sure she could see the concern on my face. "There has been a fire in your flat, but your mom and Tina are fine" she said. By this time, I started to cry. I asked, "where are they?" She stated my mom was upstairs with the police and my daughter was with my neighbors that lived in the flat below ours.

I hurried upstairs praying that my mom was okay. As I looked around, the first thing I noticed was a pile of rubble, charred from fire, on our dining room floor. As I hurried to see my mom and the policemen that were talking in the other room, I looked at my mom who was in disarray, looking so very confused with sweat pouring down her face. One policeman told me my mom had put books, papers and clothing in a pile and set them on fire.

Thoughts raced through my head of the horrible outcome that could have been. If my neighbor across the street had not seen the smoke, my mom, daughter, and possibly the family below us could have all perished while I was at work. But I didn't have time to dwell. My mother was in crisis and needed medical attention. This was not the first episode that had occurred with her mental illness since I moved in with her either. If she did not take her medicine, she would get depressed and lapse into that state.

I didn't have a car, so I asked both policemen that were there if they could help me to get my mom to the hospital to be admitted for observation of her condition.

Unfortunately, they said that they could not transport anyone unless they were taking them to jail. Tears uncontrollably burst out of my eyes and streamed down my cheeks. The weight of the situation and the hopelessness I felt for Mom nearly brought me to my knees. I begged for help and, to my surprise, just as quickly as they told me they could do nothing for us, they agreed to take us to the hospital. It was as if God had touched the minds and hearts of those police officers and persuaded them to change their decision from a *no* to a *yes*. My heart was relieved instantaneously.

I asked the neighbor downstairs if she could care for my daughter until I returned from the hospital. I did not know how long I would be since I would have to catch the bus home. My neighbor assured me she would take care of my daughter and I was ever so grateful.

My mind kept going at warp speed. My next thought was that I would need a babysitter until my mom was well so I would not lose my job. On second thought, maybe I needed to talk with my sisters and Aunt to see if they thought Mom would be okay to babysit after that episode. But then I reminded myself to take things one step at a time. Just be grateful that this situation was not as bad as it could have been.

My mom got the help that she needed and came home after about a month of treatment. I did get a babysitter to take the stress off Mom and continued to work at my job for the next 10 years. By then, I was married and had a son too. You may not be able to see the light at the end of the tunnel when you're going through tough times, but it's amazing how you can look back and see major change in your life year-over-year, month-over-month, or even day-by-day. I can see how God was, and still is, intervening in my life through every situation, and I am so grateful for Him.

"THE APOLOGY"

by Penny Duncan Stephens

Just last week, my daughter handed me an envelope and said, "Dad asked me to give you this form to fill out to help him get his full disability from the military. He needs a letter listing all the things that he did to you, or at least those that you can remember—no matter how bad—when you were married. He is trying to get the military to grant him full disability due to PTSD from the time he spent in Vietnam."

My husband, Kapp, and I were married for five years, about four of which were full of unhappiness, so I had just blotted them out of my mind—*out of sight, out of mind* as the saying goes. However, from time to time, I tend to reminisce about the love that we had for each other. Kapp was my first husband and the father of my son, who is now 43 years old. My son is the spitting image of his father. He walks, talks, and has the same mannerisms as his father. That alone sends my mind briefly back to the time Kapp and I spent together as husband and wife. From the very start, I was head over heels in love with that handsome man. He had a beautiful, dark complexion with Indian features, coal black wavy hair, and an undeniable charm that drew me in to him and fostered our unwavering love for each other. Unfortunately, love is not always enough.

Recalling those rocky years of marriage is still very painful for me. It's not something that I am willing to easily rekindle in my mind. I thought I was through with remembering all the pain and secrets of a disheveled marriage, yet I can't help but keep rewinding and replaying our life together, scene-by-scene, in the depths of my mind.

I had my first child at age 16, which made me skip ahead of those wonderful teenage years of enjoying school, basketball, football games, dating boys, and being young and free at heart. I was certainly not ready for all that was forcing me into motherhood and adulthood.

Getting engaged to Kapp at 19, I thought my life could not have been better. I was on cloud nine. I felt like this time in my life could erase all of the past guilt and shame I had experienced for years. My husband-to-be was amazing. He even promised to adopt my daughter and give her his last name. I was elated that my life was shaping up for the better. Contrary to the many words from my adopted mother, who told me I would never be anything and I was "not worth the salt in my bread." Those words still ring in my head from time to time.

Let me back up a little. After graduation from high school, I got my first real job at a store called Kresge, a five and dime store in Highland Park, Michigan. I was proud to be hired as a full-time cashier. When I was at work, my mother cared for my daughter, who was now about one and a half years of age by then. I worked four to six days a week, depending on the schedule. One day, I was checking out a line of customers and I looked over their heads to see a familiar face from the past. This man was zipping through the store, and I thought to myself wondering who it was. Then, I remembered—it was "handsome Kapp" from high school.

As he passed by, I said "I am surprised to see you in here."

He replied "I'm here on leave—had to pick up a few things. I'm scheduled to go to Vietnam in about a week or so."

Kapp and I were in several of the same classes in high school. He was very smart too. I'm pretty sure I copied answers off his paper a few times. Actually, he would push his paper to the edge of his desk, so I could see his answers. I was so appreciative of his help—he was such a gentleman.

Back in high school, Kapp was an item with a girl in our class that I was friends with also. Mary was a beautiful girl, and she too was in several of my classes. I admired their courtship, as they always seemed like a happy couple. Dating was not even on my radar back then though. I was trying to graduate on time while working a co-op job after my classes, and then I'd run back home to care for my little one. I couldn't afford to spend any extra time out after work. I had to give my mother a break from caring for my daughter all day while I was away. I know that wasn't easy on her.

The same day I noticed Kapp in the store, he finished shopping and came right up to my register. "What time do you get off?" he asked me.

"Nine" I replied, casually.

"Well, can I pick you up?" He asked, "do you have a ride home?"

I was shocked that he asked, but I answered right away. "No, I don't"

"I will pick you up at 9 then," he replied, confidently.

I told him what entrance I would be at waiting for him, but all I could think about was how he was the most handsome guy that I'd ever seen. I was so excited that he was going to pick me up in just an hour or so.

When I asked what had happened to Mary, he told me they broke up right after graduation. Kapp said for me to look out for him in a blue Lincoln Continental. *Wait, a Continental?* I said in my head. That was a "status car"—a luxury one—and my chariot home for the night. I was ecstatic to say the least—it was my time, and what an opportunity it was for me.

I remember having a huge argument the night before with the guy I was dating. He usually would pick me up from work, but since we were not talking to each other, I was planning to catch the bus home that night. However, I knew the unexpected offer from that very, very handsome guy, Kapp, was sure to change my destiny. I was ready.

As the night progressed, I was feeling giddy and excited, anticipating what was to come. I could hardly wait for my ride home with Kapp, the handsome, young guy I had not seen in almost over a year. I was so excited. But, to my surprise, when I got off work and walked outside to meet Kapp, I was stunned to see that my boyfriend had come to pick me up even though we weren't speaking. When I saw Kapp's Lincoln pull up, I acted as if I had not seen my boyfriend and hopped right in the Lincoln. I knew when my boyfriend got in touch, he would have some choice words for me since I didn't acknowledge him. Frankly, however, I no longer cared what he thought. I had bigger fish to fry!

When I got in the car, I asked Kapp if we could go somewhere to talk, and we did. I called my mother to let her know that I would be a little late, and the rest was like my ex-boyfriend—history. Kapp and I started dating a few weeks before he was deployed to Vietnam, and our attraction just blossomed. We vowed to be true to our love and commit ourselves to each other through thick and thin. Kapp had less than two years to finish his time in the service, and we were in our relationship for the long haul.

We were married six months before he ended his stint in the military. Towards the end of his time in Vietnam he would write me to say he did not know how he would cope, coming home from such a horrifying war. He said, "I have been killing people, hiding in foxholes, walking through swamps, and witnessing women and children being killed right before my eyes." He asked, "How will I ever live in civilization again?"

It was clear Kapp was tormented from having served in the Vietnam war, but I ignored his pleas for help. My focus at the time was that my man was finally coming home to me. We were going to be married and live happily ever after. My head was in the clouds. All I could think was, *is this really happening to me? I'm going to be a part of a real family as soon as he gets out—a mother, father, and child.*

Kapp came home and I hoped with every fiber of my being that my fantasy of a wonderful, loving family would play out. After we were married about a year, my son was born into our union. Unfortunately, however, our marriage only lasted about five years and that was the story of us.

Filling out the paperwork for Kapp's Veterans Affairs claim had brought back so many painful memories. When I started, I had no idea that going back to this period in my life would hurt so badly. It was very, very painful. Kapp had a severe case of PTSD, which, although I had heard about the condition, I really did not understand much about it. As I went through the paperwork, I could hear my daughter's voice in my head saying, "mom as much as you can remember, no matter how bad, please answer the questions related to the topics and return to daddy as soon as possible." I may not have understood PTSD, but I knew Kapp needed my help, or he wouldn't have asked, so I did the best I could to respond.

There were several topics and disorders for me to write about. I felt I needed to get the meaning of each disorder listed, so I could write to each one effectively. One quality about me is that if I'm going to do something, I want to do it to the best of my ability. The topics listed were—delusional behavior, generalized anxiety disorder, post-traumatic stress disorder, and depersonalization disorder. After recalling the incidents that had occurred during our marriage in my mind, it seemed his behavior had shown symptoms of each of those disorders. I felt guilty for being totally oblivious to the signs and feeling that I was a victim of the circumstances. I had been selfish. I was only thinking of me.

After seeing that his actions were so identical to each disorder that I was writing about, I felt hollow knowing that I believed that each one of our altercations was personal—a personal attack directed right at me. I wondered how I could continue to live through it all or how I could get out of my marriage. While I was experiencing so much pain from what was going on, I never once thought about what he might be going through.

While I was pregnant with my son, I would suddenly find myself on the floor in total dismay after being kicked with full force out of a sound sleep. I remember looking up, screaming at him from the floor, yelling, "What is going on?" Each time he did it, he would quickly explain in an apologetic voice, "I'm sorry. I had a nightmare, I thought you were the enemy and I had to get you out of my foxhole." When it happened again, I started sleeping in the spare bedroom. I felt it would be safer for me and my son.

Kapp was suffering badly from PTSD. At the time, I did not have the slightest clue what my husband was going through. I didn't realize that he needed help. I was so young and green. I had gone through so much in my childhood that I could not see the forest for the trees. The only thing I could say to him right now: *I apologize.*

Now, I think about what our young men go through in various wars fighting for our country. They go through hell and back. What they endure, only to be rejected for medical attention and counseling many times after they have gone through so much, is too much for any person to bear.

I'm not going to tell you all that I went through at this time. I'll save some for another chapter. I believe my husband's actions were a direct result of what he experienced in the Vietnam War. God, please help all our veterans. And, God, thank you for the awakening in my life to no longer be the "victim" and to gain the knowledge to understand what had happened between my ex-husband and me.

Even though I went through a lot and lost my marriage of five years, I survived. With help, I am an overcomer. I hope my responses to the Veterans Affairs questionnaire help Kapp get the amount of care he deserves. What happened to my husband and thousands of other veterans is horrible and unacceptable. Even though reliving that period in my life was an uncomfortable experience, I feel that there was a purpose in all of it because it helped me to grow and understand so much more about PTSD. I pray for an end to all wars.

I finally called Kapp and apologized after all these years. I told him that I wished I had understood that he needed my help, professional counseling, and medical attention. He accepted my apology and assured me that he understood that I really did not know what was going on, because he didn't know either. I am so appreciative to have gained this knowledge—even this late. I felt another layer of the onion being peeled back so to speak—a heavy burden lifted off me.

Thank you, God, for bringing this to the forefront of my awareness.

LIFE IS A PRECIOUS, UNIQUE, GIFT:

THE FORBIDDEN WORD

by Inez T. Thomas

I grew up in Middle Georgia in the early 1950s. Back then, segregation was the norm. Our house was five miles outside the city limits. The homes in my neighborhood were approximately one mile apart. Everyone knew each other in the community either through church, school, or from working in the fields. Any adult in the community would chastise you if they thought you were doing something wrong. Once your parents were notified of your indiscretion, they would discipline you too. There were 10 families in our neighborhood. The general store was called W.M. Fosters. It was located off GA Highway 80 approximately a half mile north of our house. Highway 80 was the main gateway from Atlanta to Dublin, Georgia. Running parallel to the highway were the railroad tracks. The railroad and Highway 80 were the two ways of travel. The largest employer of the county was Georgia Kaolin and Company. Middle Georgia was rich in the mineral chalk, and Georgia Kaolin and Company excavated chalk from the ground. They manufactured sheet rock and many other paper products. A lot of us kids ate the white chalk. The Kaolin plant operated 24 hours a day. They had three shifts. Most mornings the men from the third shift would congregate at the store to catch up on all the latest gossip.

At this time my family consisted of five older siblings— four girls and one boy. My twin sister, Trunell, and I were the babies. We were five years old. My grandmother, Inez, better known as "Big Mom," would take us to our neighbor Idella's house. Mrs. Idella would babysit us while Big Mom would go to work. Mrs. Idella babysat for other children, as well. This neighborhood was located on the east side of the railroad tracks and Highway 80. On the left of Mrs. Idella's house was Mrs. Lizzie's and Mr. Frank and Mrs. Emma lived on the right. Mrs. Lizzie had seven children, including two daughters, Cal and Bugger, and a lot of grandchildren too. There was no shortage of children to play with for us.

On one summer day, we were outside playing. Trunell and I thought we saw our older sister, Mary, in the distance across the tracks. The girl walking was wearing a skirt just like the one Mary had on when she left that day. Trunell and I were convinced it was Mary, so we decided to go after her. We held hands and crossed over the railroad tracks. Then, we proceeded to cross Highway 80, being careful to look both ways for traffic first.

Once safely across the road, we were at Foster's general store. The owner, Mr. Foster, was a white man.

"Aren't you Mrs. Inez's children?" asked Mr. Foster.

We confirmed that we were. He further inquired as to why we were out crossing the road. We explained that we were following our sister. We later learned that the girl we were following was Bugger, not our sister Mary. Mr. Foster asked Ben, one of the men sitting on the store bench, to go and inform my grandmother that her children were in the road.

When Mrs. Idella realized that we weren't in the yard, she sent her son after us. When he caught up with us, I bit him, and we headed home running because we didn't want to go back to his house. We sat on the porch until my sister arrived. I remember us being in so much trouble.

When my grandmother got home, she asked why we left the babysitter's house. We tried our best to answer satisfactorily, but there was no explanation she would accept. She said, "When I take you somewhere you stay there until I pick you up! Do you understand?" She spanked us and yelled, "YOU WILL NEVER RUN AWAY

Railroad tracks near Highway 80

AGAIN." Once the spanking was over, she put us to bed and told us to take a nap. We slept together.

When we woke up from our forced nap, Trunell asked, "Inez, are you ready?"

My grandmother overheard Trunell—I can't imagine what she had assumed that meant, but she immediately picked up where she'd left off and spanked us again. That was the first and last time my grandmother gave us a spanking.

At age 50, Trunell and I went to Las Vegas to celebrate our birthdays. She lives in Colorado, and I live in Georgia. We had a magnificent time. As we were departing, we looked at each other and said, "do you think we can say run away?" We began to laugh because that was the forbidden word of our vocabulary and a lesson learned.

At the age of 60, we celebrated our birthday together again.

Twin sisters Inez and Trunell, age 60.

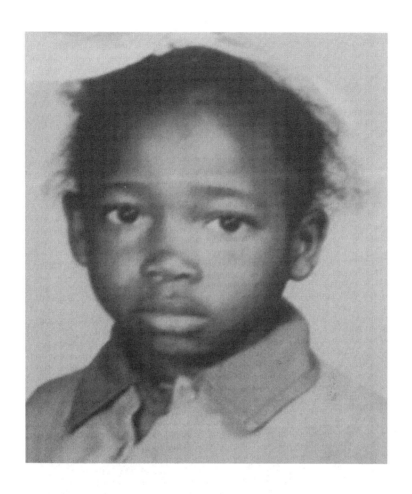

Trunell Perry

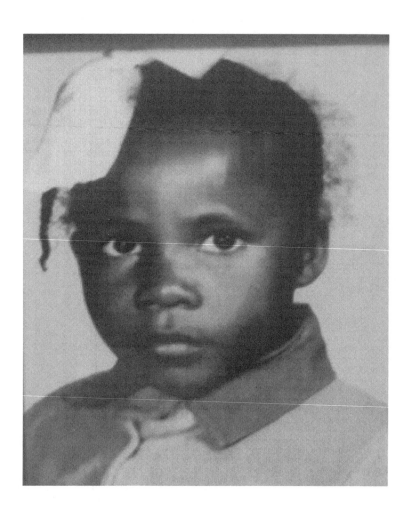

Inez T. Thomas

The word *happiness* cannot describe what we felt during our 60th birthday party. We both had "megawatt smiles" from ear to ear. We were dressed in matching sea green and ivory formfitting, lace dresses, tailored just for that magnificent occasion. Our makeup was perfect, and it emphasized our dazzling, green eyes. Our orange manicured nails were beautiful, and our fingers were adorned with our diamond wedding rings of which their sparkles could be seen for miles.

There were decorations of emerald green and ivory surrounding the event center where we held our 60th party like none have seen before. We smiled and posed on the stair-steps together, embellished in colors of coral and orange, thanking each of our guests for coming out to celebrate with us.

I am so thankful for my sister. She is always only a phone call away. I love talking to her because she is truly my best friend. The joy we share in being together makes any time we may spend apart a distant memory.

THE PERFECT HOLIDAY

by Inez T. Thomas

It was 1980 January—my first flight to Hawaii. I'd never traveled further than Florida and Ohio. My parents would typically visit relatives in these states, and I would go along with them, but I never took a trip all on my own. However, this time I was about to head to Hawaii—to live. I was so excited. I didn't know what to expect but I knew I wanted to go. My young son, who was several months old, and my husband, Horace, took the trip with me. Horace was a Marine, and he had new orders to be transferred to Kaneohe Marine Corps Air Station.

The flight was so long. We finally arrived in Hawaii after seven hours. I was so tired, yet still excited when we got off the plane. I looked around and all I could see were native Hawaiians. The men had on flowered shirts and the ladies wore pretty, long floral dresses. Everyone had beautiful colored leis around their necks. The most amazing thing that captured my attention was the size of the ladies. Coming from Georgia, I had never seen so many little people before. I immediately started tapping my husband saying, "Look, look." He stared at me like I had lost my mind.

"What's wrong with you?" he asked.

"The little ladies," I mused, "they are my size. I'm so excited I don't know what to do."

Our sponsor came up with a sign that read "Thomas" and greeted us to the island with floral leis. We headed off to the hotel. I was so happy. I thought to myself, *the first thing I'm*

Inez T. Thomas

going to do is head for the shop. The shopping was great. I was able to find dresses that fit me, and since everyone there was short just like me, I could wear flat shoes and be just as tall as all the other ladies. I was in hog heaven. Within about two weeks, the car arrived, and I had the freedom to move around, which I was thankful for because I had gotten tired of just staying in the hotel.

Horace came home from work during our first few weeks on the island and told me that he would be going on a six-month deployment. *How could this be?* I thought. *We just arrived. I don't know anyone here. We don't have any furniture. We have clothes for two weeks. How can they do this to us? What will we do? When will my household goods arrive? Where will we stay?* Those were all questions that were bombarding me, having heard that bad news.

Our son was very young. I couldn't help but wonder who would help me take care of him. The Marine Corps didn't seem to care. All I heard was that the ship would deploy the very next month, but I had to be strong and make some decisions. I wondered if I would be able to stop my household shipment from being delivered to Hawaii, and just move back to Atlanta until Horace returned from deployment. Unfortunately, I soon discovered that was not an option. We couldn't stay in the hotel indefinitely, so we had to find a place to live before he deployed in three weeks.

My life was an up and down rollercoaster for the next three weeks. On February 13th, 1980, Horace's ship departed from the port. I had a conversation with my son— as if he understood—he was far too young, but I figured I needed to tell him what was going on anyway. We both had to do some growing to survive. That day would be the day he stopped bottle feeding, I told him. It was way too hot for me to be carrying heavy bottles of milk and him. He would start potty training soon and learn to walk too. With Horace gone, we both had to be as independent as possible.

After about two months, my household shipment finally arrived. I had met a lady at the hotel where we were living, and she told me that her husband was a Marine too. She said they both would be in the area, and he would help my son and me move into our new home. Little did I know at the time, but this man was interested in more than just helping me move. He wanted to have sex with me, knowing my husband would be gone for six months. I couldn't believe it! I thought, *HAVE YOU LOST YOUR MIND!* When I spoke to other Marine wives with deployed husbands, they had similar experiences with that man. I wondered how his wife could not know what he was up to if he tried that mess with so many women. Needless to say, I ended my friendship with "Mr. Not So Helpful."

The next several months were extremely busy. I spent most of my time getting the house set up and potty training the baby. Once he was potty trained, I started to look for a job. I enrolled him in daycare, and I enrolled in The University Hawaii Continuing Education. I got a job at Schofield Barracks on the Army base. I would meet with other wives whose husbands were deployed and they were talking about receiving letters and gifts from their husbands. I didn't receive any gifts, just a few letters. I talked to my son and told him that Dad was coming home soon. I showed him pictures of his dad so he would remember him. The day of his arrival finally came. We were dressed up and looking pretty, waiting for the ship to dock. Remember, we were still newlyweds of less than three years. I was so excited. The first night home our son was so thrilled his dad was home he forgot he was potty trained and pooped on the floor behind the bathroom door.

For the next few weeks, things were a little chaotic around the house because I was used to being in control. Once Horace arrived, he wanted to change things, which created tension between us. For the next two years we had three additional six-month deployments. I didn't like them; however, I think being alone during those times made me a stronger, more well-rounded person. I got to meet a lot of new people. I learned the Hawaiian and Japanese culture. I joined Toastmistress International, and I was elected president of the NCO Wives Club. I also got pregnant a second time, but I had a miscarriage. That was a difficult experience for me, but I eventually pulled myself together after the loss of our baby. Horace finished his tour of duty in Hawaii, and we moved back to the mainland. After several more duty stations, we eventually retired to live out our lives in Atlanta.

Fast forward 30 years later, and I went back to Hawaii on vacation in 2014, accompanied by my baby sister and a high school friend. We stayed at the Waikiki Sheraton Hotel in Honolulu. We enjoyed all the tours and events. I went back to Kaneohe Bay to my old home in Pearl City. Everything looked similar but different. I didn't really have all the time to explore the area like I did when I lived there, but I enjoyed the experience of revisiting my home away from home and I did lots of shopping. I shipped all the items I purchased back to Atlanta through the mail. I finally got to enjoy the Polynesian Culture Center and Pearl Harbor, which I had wanted to see when I lived there. Back then, I didn't get to experience those places because our son was too small, and I was not allowed to take him there. I must say I really enjoyed living in Hawaii, and I was glad I had a chance to go back and visit years later.

IS IT THE FUNERAL OR THE FOOD?

by Inez T. Thomas

Mount Zion Church is located at the center of Georgia, approximately 100 miles south of Atlanta. The church's congregation is of African American descent. It sits on 25 acres of land and half of the land is designated for burial. Any member or non-member of the community can be buried in the church's cemetery free of charge. It has become a popular place for burials since most churches require a $500 fee to bury someone. The church was built 139 years ago, and my grandfather was one of its original members. He and my grandmother had 10 children, eight boys and two girls. All their children joined the church; therefore, membership was the norm for the entire family. To say it is a family church is an understatement. There are five predominant family histories associated with Mount Zion Church.

The church always provides meat—usually chicken—for each repast. Family and friends bring everything else. Everyone in the community knows which families provide the "good" food. When a member of one of those families passes, the church is always at full capacity. There is never a shortage of volunteers working in the kitchen. The church's kitchen committee usually consists of the deaconess and seven women from the church. They make up the menu and bring their own Tupperware containers to take their meal before the mourning family has a chance to eat. Though many members will bring food to share, surprisingly, there is always a crew who do not. They're called the "eat them up crew" because they don't bring anything but will carry out all of the leftovers for "grandma who is at home in the wheelchair and can't come."

It amazes me how we as individuals get so excited about food. It can be simple things, like pigtails in collard greens that Cousin Juicy made. Or even the cake that Sarah made, as you slice three pieces of your own before you can even serve the people.

Well, Mamie says before you start to prepare the plates, "Let's take out our chicken and put it under the counter, because we got to eat too." The pastor has a table set aside for him and his staff. There is a dedicated server for his table. She will begin by saying, "You know those greens and homemade cake should be on his table. But, girl, wait. Didn't Sarah make that lemon pound cake? Let me taste a piece because you know my sugar is down." The server would down a piece of cake, exclaim, "wow, that was good," and get right back to business. "Juicy, are you through with them greens? Please put the entire pigtail on a plate. We'll eat them with cornbread later over at Momma's house after church."

The ladies would continue to work until everything was done. The main server would say, "The plates are done. How many do we have? 375? That is just enough. Well, Cora, take your stuff to the car, so these nosy people won't be looking. If all else fails, we have some vegetables and cake to hold them over. We aren't trying to fill them up, just a little something to 'tide them over' until they get home."

If the funeral service tends to last longer than normal, guests will excuse themselves with two fingers held above their head, heading towards the kitchen for a plate to go. They tend to ask for additional plates with chicken breast for family members who are not in attendance.

The question remains, "did they come to support the family, or did they come for the food?"

THAT'S ME

By Inez T. Thomas

If I have to tell you one more time to hurry up, I am going to slap you silly, I thought. Why do you do this? I told you yesterday we were leaving at nine o'clock this morning. What do I see? You are sitting on the side of the bed saying give me five more minutes. I keep telling myself that I am not taking you to any more doctors' appointments. You have gotten on my last nerve. I can't go through this again this year. I must have a big "S" on my forehead because you know I'll continue to take you. By the time we get there they'll be ready to commit me too because my blood pressure will be 270/150, my blood sugar will be 200, and I'll be dripping wet from sweating. I am so angry. Have I lost my mind?

I'll just run away from home. I look at myself in the mirror and say maybe, "You did marry him twice." I smile and think how young we were. Back then, I had been so frustrated at my job of five years that I was ready to quit. I had made the ultimate mistake; I dipped my pen in the company's ink. I had a relationship with a co-worker—the first and last time I ever let that happen. It was a very hard lesson to learn—one with an everlasting effect. I needed a career change. *Why not the military?* I thought. I could travel and see the world. I thought that would be the perfect job to have, so I put in my application and waited for a recruiter to show up. As it turns out, Horace was the recruiter. He was so handsome in his Marine uniform, and I was instantly attracted to him.

During that home visit, Horace reviewed my qualifications, and with a hundred-watt smile said, "I'll have to get you a height waiver, or the other option is that you could marry me and travel."

Six months later we got married. Being a military wife was hard. We moved 12 times across four different states, and my husband experienced deployments, wars, depression, disappointments, and post-traumatic stress disorder. We endured long separations and even got divorced once, just to name a few challenges. I was a broken woman, mentally and physically. Nevertheless, had I not gone through those hardships and difficult experiences, I would not be the loving, caring, kind and nurturing person that I am today. I look back and classify all those experiences as learning tools.

My husband went through a lot. Today, he doesn't have a six pack, he's legally blind, and he doesn't drive. He is stubborn, moves slowly, and does no chores. But, with all of that said, after 37 years, I still love him.

I contribute a lot of who I am to my humble beginnings. I was born in Georgia during segregation. I am the sixth child of eight. There were seven girls and one boy. I have a fraternal twin sister and I am the eldest by six minutes. The house we grew up in still stands today. Fifty-five years ago, it didn't have indoor plumbing, gas, or electricity. I attended Twiggs County High School and several colleges and received many years of training while working at the Department of Transportation (FAA) and the Department of Defense. Most of my studies were in avionics, communications, electronics, and navigation. I have worked for 35 years in various positions, including Avionics Instruments Technician, Airways Transportation System Specialist, Airborne Electronics Technician, and Flight Inspections Mission Specialist.

I remember achieving one of my greatest accomplishments in 1999 when I became the first and only black woman in the United States to hold the position of an Airborne Electronics Technician. I flew around the country in a specially equipped Beechcraft 300 and a Learjet aircraft, inspecting communications and navigational aids, a task better known as a "Flight Check".

My grandmother, Inez, who I was named after, had a profound impact on my life. She was born March 21st, 1900. She lived to be 89 years old before the Lord took her home. She was a saved religious woman who believed in prayer. She taught me to cook, to sew, and good work ethics. My grandmother would take my twin sister, Trunell, and me to work in the fields, picking cotton, peas, and beans. My main chores growing up were to gather firewood, eggs from the hen house, and water from the spring each day.

My first introduction to God and the Bible was through my grandmother. She would sing spiritual songs and pray as we worked. On one occasion, she explained that she was not given the opportunity to go to school, so she couldn't read or write. She encouraged us to study hard and learn everything we could. She said that education was a possession that could not be taken away once you acquired it.

We lived next door to Grandmother and would go to her house to read the Bible. Even though she was not book-learned, she was wise and showed love to everyone. She was anointed with the Holy Ghost and had the gift of speaking in tongue. When we read the Bible to her, she would explain what the Lord was saying in the scripture. She eventually learned to read some. Throughout my childhood, and even through my son's early years, she would give each child a dollar every month from her social security check. This was a grandmother's love—the first true love I can remember. I love my grandmother and I still think of her often.

I honestly love my life today. My husband and I have one son and two grandchildren. We are both retired and spend most weekends together at home doing absolutely nothing. Without realizing it, I had started my spiritual transformation. I never lost my faith in God. I know He loved me when I didn't love myself. Today, I pray for patience because God has truly blessed me and my family. So, whatever time He gives me, I am going to accept it as a great gift without complaint.

LOVING AND BEING LOVED

by Debora Starr

"And now these three remain: faith, hope and love. But the greatest of these is LOVE" (King James Version, 1 Corinthians 13:13).

When I was young and the world was an easier place to be, I envisioned myself at age 50. I would see myself wearing a size 12 dress and I'd have a nice-sized bank account, a wonderful husband, a perfect

home in an upscale neighborhood, and the ability to do extremely nice things for my mother and aunt. Everything would just be peachy keen. Back then in my mind, I did not see and, in my heart, did not believe that things would end up how they did. This was just the way the world was made and my place in it. In my eyes, I refused to see those two ladies aging. I saw myself aging very nicely, but not the two people who had been the bulwarks in my life.

The year was 1999. It was an early summer day in Atlanta. The weather was hot but not as hot as it would soon be. Every conversation I heard about the weather that day began with "it sure is hot." The sky was blue with just a few clouds, and it was time for me to go home. I emerged from my cubicle on time that day. It was not uncommon for me to linger at work to handle some long-winded project that I had been assigned. Often, I did not mind donating the extra time, because the project had been assigned to me, and I could work on it without being interrupted by the normal office hoopla coming from bosses, co-workers, telephone calls, and other activities which had nothing to do with actual work. But that day, I walked to my car in the parking lot with an important and different destination on my mind.

I drove along the access road of the expressway on I-75 many times. Depending on where you wanted to get off the expressway, you could ride along the access roads and merge back into the regular traffic going south. I was going south, which saved a few minutes—maybe. It certainly saved a little stress because I was on the expressway versus a slow-moving traffic jam on the streets of Atlanta that could extend in every direction about forty miles outside of the city. Riding along the access road, I had more time to think about my next move. Having traveled along the road from work to home so frequently, I knew which lane to get into, when to get into the lane, and how many minutes it would take to get where I was going. My mind and my driving automatically adjusted to the conditions on the road, which were typically jam packed. Not only was I riding parallel to the regular traffic, but my mind was also running parallel to what was happening. I felt like I was having an out-of-body experience. I cannot remember what I was wearing, but I remember being in a normal traffic jam, and yet I was not in it. I was moving towards my destination adjacent to the traffic with my mind on what I would find at the destination. I remember the clear blue sky in front of me. I was staring at the distant horizon, moving forward, as that was the only way to go. Someone special at my destination needed me and, even if I wanted to avoid what was coming, there was no way to stand still or go backwards.

Aunt Mary had been my "defensive back" all my life. Sometimes, when I try to describe her spirit, I say that she was one of those angels flying too close to the ground. I grew up knowing that Aunt Mary was considered a very good-looking woman. She had curly hair that would arrange itself into nappy, curly ringlets if she left it alone and didn't try to straighten it. You know, the people that we now call "black" come in all shades, and we have names for every shade. Aunt Mary had reddish brown skin, that some people in the Black community might call, "paper sack brown," except hers had definite red undertones. Her skin was so smooth and hairless that if you touched her, you would be surprised at its baby smooth texture. She was about five foot ten, according to her own description, and she was big boned without an extra ounce of fat. She wasn't thin or fat. She just had a sturdy frame. Now, mind you, I will forever see her face in my mind's eye, but her physical characteristics came to be such a secondary attribute that once I understood who she really was, I did not see or care about her hair, her skin, her height, her weight, or any other physical attributes. She was Aunt Mary and that was all that was important. She was one of those people who was so right with the world—her embodiment of human form was just a necessity. She was like pure sugar with a dose of reality.

Aunt Mary did not have any children, but she was mine, and I was hers. As a matter of fact, people who did not know better, could not tell if she was my birth mother or not, even though I did not look like her at all. The synergy between the two of us was such that we just looked like we were together. We could communicate with each other without saying a word, and usually those telepathic conversations were about topics that defy words. Whether words were used or not, if I had a problem that I was trying to figure out, if I took it to Aunt Mary, I knew that I was going to be taught and protected with a firm and gentle spirit. We could look into each other's eyes and rejoice at the good outcome of a situation, or we could cry together with neither of us shedding a tear. The conversation was all in the meeting of the eyes and soul.

All my life, Aunt Mary has lived with Mama and me, but I am still not saying it right. A better description of my relationship with Aunt Mary is a name that would slip from my lips when I was in a hurry to speak to her. Rather than saying "Aunt Mary", I would call her Ma-Aunt Mary. What

I meant to say was "Aunt Mary." Out of respect to Mama, I did not call Aunt Mary "Mama", but what slipped out of my mouth was an accurate and appropriate name for the relationship, Ma-Aunt Mary. She was one of my Mama's but technically she was Aunt Mary.

The three of us lived together from the time I was born and brought home from the city hospital until I got my own apartment after college. As a young child, I remember how I celebrated her arrival on our street after she returned from work and had gotten off the bus. I would dance and jump up and down and cheer "Aunt Mary, Aunt Mary, Aunt Mary!" If you did not know better you would think that I was cheering a parade—Santa Claus, the tooth fairy— or that I had seen someone that I hadn't seen for a long time. I cheered for her arrival home like she was a celebrity. When she walked up onto the porch, I hugged her around her knees, and she just smiled. Looking back on it, I imagine it made her feel loved to have a child celebrate her return home from work the way I did.

Mama, with Aunt Mary's help, was an unbelievable provider. At that time, we lived in one of the most well-known inner-city ghettos in Atlanta called Vine City. My clothes came from everywhere—the Salvation Army, hand-me-downs from my mother's employer, Miss Betty, a doctor's wife, discount stores like Sunshine's, and from exclusive shops like Leon-Froshin and J. P. Allen. They were never cheap or of poor quality. We lived in the city, but Mama and Aunt Mary were country women who knew exactly what to do in the kitchen. Mama had a garden in the backyard on a lot that was probably less than a quarter of an acre. Just as with the clothes, they knew how to shop for bargains on food and everything else we needed. The two of them taught me to be frugal but to be aware of quality. Our household never had store bought snacks. We always had homemade cookies and cakes, vegetables, and meat. We had what we needed, but no junk food whatsoever.

Mama and Aunt Mary were both disciplinarians with different styles of getting their point across. Mama was laser-focused when moving towards whatever goal she had in mind. She had the stern persona of a "no nonsense, no pampering, stop crying, get up and do what I say do" icon. I had to be a fully-grown woman to recognize that she had frailties and flaws just like every other human being, and that she was just as kind as Aunt Mary. But Mama had a plan, and that plan was that one day her only child would not have to live in Vine City. Her focus dictated that I go to school, finish college, and support myself. Mama knew just how to keep me scared enough of her that I would rather do almost anything but disappoint her. Aunt Mary had a different way about her. She knew how to get inside your head and get you to do things her way without hurting your feelings. When she got through soothing you and giving you an opportunity to implement "our plan," you felt like you came up with the idea yourself, or at least you had achieved a compromise on the house rules. If you requested something of Mama that she was not going to do, or did not want you to do, the answer would be a clear "no." However, on the same topic with the same answer, Aunt Mary's reply would start something like, "Debora, I am going to help you do it like this. I am going to be right here with you." Two very different styles.

I loved school and books when I was a child which fell right into Mama's plans. Mama and Aunt Mary expected A's on my report card; B's were acceptable, but I needed to have more A's than B's. I never got a C, thank Heaven. What you need to know is Aunt Mary stayed up with me until all my homework was done. If it was math that I had to do, we did it together. If it was a paper that I had to write, she would listen to me read it when I finished writing no matter the subject. She remained with me until I had the confidence to complete the assignment, and it did not matter how long it took. She did this with me from elementary school through high school, and I would read my college papers to her.

Transistor radios were all the rage when I was about ten years old. I wanted a transistor radio for Christmas, so I asked Mama for one. Her answer was no. Now understand that we lived frugally, but not deprived, and Mama could have gotten the transistor radio for me for Christmas.

Mama was not affected by "what the Joneses had." I really don't know why she would not get a radio. More than likely Mama had budgeted what she wanted to spend for Christmas. Mama's answer was no, and that was the end of the conversation with her. No amount of crying, pleading, begging, talking, or anything else was going to change her mind. But guess what? I got a transistor radio for Christmas. That's right. The radio was Aunt Mary's gift to me.

The transistor radio episode was the first time I remember Aunt Mary running interference for me to soften what appeared to be Mama's unforgiving offense to keep me focused. That was the first time I can really remember Aunt Mary stepping in to save me. Aunt Mary was my protector until the day she died. It really did not matter who you were, who you thought you were, or how big you were, you were going to have to go through her to get to do anything hurtful to me.

I started to work when I was thirteen at the neighborhood grocery store. Somehow, I managed to continue working until I retired. I would say that from age thirteen until retirement, I worked without having as many as six months being unemployed. I was employed during all of college, and in my last year, I asked Mama if I could get a car. Mama's answer was no. Now, I really don't understand what was behind that decision, but all my life we had never had a car. I just thought, *I'm working. I have almost finished school, and I make enough money to do this myself.* I would never ask Mama to buy a car for me. To ask your parent(s) to buy a car for you was unheard of when I was young. You were supposed to get your own car or keep riding the bus or catching a ride with someone who had a car. I did not expect Aunt Mary to run interference for me on this one. I just continued to try to convince Mama. Now, I don't know what type of conversations they may have had about a car when I wasn't around, but I don't remember Aunt Mary saying anything to me or Mama on the subject. One day, when Mama went to work, Aunt Mary suggested we catch the bus and go downtown on Peachtree to the Hub Ford car lot. There really wasn't much haggling over the price of the car. Now I realize that what took all day long to negotiate a price was a fair deal and a done deal in a short period of time. We prepared to leave the car lot in my new one-year-old, baby blue Mercury Montego. And no! Aunt Mary did not buy the car for me. Maybe she could have, but she did not. What she did was help to negotiate a price and the terms. She anteed up the down payment so that the salesman sold the car to me on her terms. It was my car and in my name. As a family, we did not believe in co-signing for anything. That was one of my first lessons as a young adult: learning what a little money can do if you know the power of cash and how to negotiate. It is a lesson that I have used all my life.

I could write an encyclopedia trying to tell you how Aunt Mary demonstrated her love for me over, and over, and over again. If you have ever had this kind of connection with a person that words cannot express, you know that something is going on that you can feel, but you cannot ever fully describe. If you have ever been loved unconditionally, as she loved me, you know that it doesn't happen often in a lifetime.

So, one afternoon when I was on my way to the nursing home, I remember thinking, *I must get to where Aunt Mary is to look in her face....to make certain that she is okay. I loved her so much that I rather not deal with this situation. But this is what I must do, and it is the best I can do right now.* I picked Mama up—I had to—we were a set of three, and it just did not make sense to leave Mama out to be wondering how Aunt Mary was doing. Now that I think about it, we all had a way of being watchful and silently figuring out the next move together, and I do mean together. If I did not pick her up and take her with me, it only meant that I would have to go back home and try to tell her what I saw, or I would have to try to convince her that her only sister, with whom she had lived about 90% of her life with, was alright. If Aunt Mary was not alright, I would have to tell her something else, and it was just best to let her see for herself.

Aunt Mary was about 90 years old now. What I learned about aging was more than what I wanted to know or accept—albeit her aging was graceful. Aunt Mary had fallen and broken her hip. The doctor said that it was hard to know if the hip broke and then she fell because of it. All I knew was that I had just left their high rise, and shortly after I opened the door and stepped inside my house, I heard the phone ring. It was Aunt Mary on the other end, almost shouting. After all the years of hearing her voice, I had never heard this screaming tone come from her.

"Debora, I fell!" The words sounded to have tears dripping off them. Aunt Mary was not a person that ever cried for herself. I had watched her patiently go through many illnesses, but I had never heard that pitiful tone.

"I'll be there in a minute," I replied.

"Okay," she said.

Aunt Mary had fallen in the hall walking back from Mama's apartment. Somehow, by the time I arrived, Aunt Mary was in her bed. At that time, I did not believe that her hip was broken. I guess you could say that I have always been an optimist. I have a bad habit of fighting for whatever I want and hoping for the best outcome. On that night, at about 11:00 p.m., I asked Aunt Mary to stay in her bed. I told her that I would check on her the next morning. A broken hip was not on my radar. Optimism and naivety had me hoping that she was just bruised and shook-up, but I was wrong. The next day I took her to the doctor, and it was a broken hip.

The next week was awful. I found out that you must wait for a broken hip to heal. Mama tried her best to take care of Aunt Mary. Of course, I would take over when I got off work and try to make certain that they both were alright. All three of us tried to take care of each other without any question of what would have to be done. However, the plan did not work for Mama to help Aunt Mary while I was at work. First, Mama could barely walk herself. Osteoporosis had wrecked her limbs, and if that was not bad enough, she had a previous digestive operation that left her fighting for every ounce of food and weight. Secondly, Aunt Mary and Mama fought like cats and dogs even though they were inseparable. If you were around them, you just had to suffer through it. And you better not take sides, try to calm them down, or interject any thoughts on the subject because you would incur the wrath of both.

There was Aunt Mary who basically could not do anything for herself, and Mama who could barely take care of herself - both at home during the day while I was at work. By the time I would get to their high-rise after work, you could cut the tension in the air with a knife. If the dictionary had pictures of "sibling arguments" and "sun-downing," Mama and Aunt Mary's faces would be on the page. By the way, *sun-downing* is a word I learned as a result of trying to help them. It means that it can take so much effort for an older person to perform normal tasks to get through a day—they get tired and cranky, just like children.

When I would walk through the door, eyes would be rolling back and forth, and Mama would start on her speech which was nonstop until she cooled off the next day—that is, unless something else would make her angry. Mama could make such a fuss that it was always better to get a whipping or a spanking. Aunt Mary and I would just suffer through her diatribe until she cooled off or Aunt Mary got tired of listening to her rant. But that's another story. I don't think I will ever meet anyone kinder than my Aunt Mary, but if you made her mad, she could cuss in six different languages in one sentence—she stuttered too. To be with Aunt Mary when she got upset was like watching a dormant volcano erupt, but she did not hold a grudge and she would help you fix whatever problem you had. She might say, "I mean for you to shut up and shut up now, Lula Belle. Damnit." Mama would fuss a little while longer, and then the whole conversation would just sputter into a silence that transformed the fight into normal household activities.

During the days after Aunt Mary had fallen, when I arrived at their high-rise, I could tell that they had had one of their epic battles. There was a new kind of sick quietness thrown over the apartment like a starting-to-sour wet blanket. It broke my heart to see Aunt Mary confined to a chair while Mama berated her. It was not because Aunt Mary had done something wrong, but because Mama was tired, cranky, and trying to help her sister although Mama could barely help herself. My heart sank. I could not stand to watch it. These two women, together, had been so self-sufficient up until that point in their lives.

I asked Aunt Mary if she would go to the nursing home for a week for rehab. That would give her a chance to get stronger. The three of us had a family policy to cooperate for the unit to move past "stuck" and as kind, gentle, and sweet as she was, she said "okay." That is how Aunt Mary got to the nursing home in the first place.

Now there I was, driving down I-75 often. First, I would pick up Mama and then we would go to the nursing home to see my dear Aunt Mary. By nature, I would say that I am quietly watchful while I try to figure out what I need to do to help make the best of a situation. I would want to know if she was being treated well, if she was clean and dry, if she was hungry, and if she was lonely. I wanted to know if my Aunt Mary was alright. When I got there, Aunt Mary was not in the room where she had been the previous day. The nursing assistant showed us to Aunt Mary's new room. However, the strangest thing was that she was trying to explain to us that some man had assaulted her and that she had fought him off as hard as she could. We knew that her account of an assault in the nursing home had not happened, but Mama and I looked at each other. We did not say a word. We were trying to figure out what was going on.

Mama and I could tell that Aunt Mary had not been physically hurt so we did not want to cause an unpleasant scene in the nursing home. We asked why she was moved, and the nurse muttered something about Aunt Mary and the other resident in the room not getting along. But I knew right away that the nurse's account was not exactly a true one. I remember leaving Aunt Mary in the room with a white woman. The white woman had been assigned to the room first. Let's just be clear, something racial went on and Aunt Mary probably gave that woman a piece of her mind in one of her special six languages she used. Aunt Mary was kinder than anyone else I knew on this earth, but she did have a fiery personality when it came to not putting up with nonsense. When we found Aunt Mary, what she said was more disturbing than getting to that home and not finding her where she was supposed to be.

We stayed with Aunt Mary for about an hour. With all three of us there, she began to calm down. When we were certain that the episode, whatever it was, was over, we prepared to leave. Walking out of that room and getting in the car put heaviness on our hearts like a soaking wet towel. The truth is Mama could barely take care of herself with my assistance, and she certainly could not take care of Aunt Mary, and I had to go to work. There are a lot of things in life that you don't like, and for me this was one of the worst things I had to do. I had to choose to keep a roof over my head and finish out a few years before I retired or leave my aunt at the nursing home. *Lord, have mercy.*

I got Mama back to her high-rise, and I stayed there for a few minutes to get her settled in before heading home. I came up with the plan to visit Aunt Mary every day. God had sent that plan to me. You know, if you have a loved one in a nursing home, you almost have to go every day. It's just the nature of the beast. So, I went every day, as it wasn't far from my house. It added a couple of hours to my daily routine. I grew more comfortable with the nursing home situation, and the idea of it soothed Aunt Mary. I knew that she was looking for me, but sometimes she would say, "It is time for you to go home, it's cold, it's getting late, or traffic is bad out there and you need to go home." Can you imagine anyone loving a person that much? Aunt Mary was in a wheelchair, living in a nursing home, quite frail, and sometimes very sick, but if you tried to hurt me, her Debora, she would have stood up, walked over to you, and slapped you silly.

This situation went on for about a year and a half. I would take Mama to see Aunt Mary and get her out of the nursing home on the weekends. I would also bring Mama to my house and get Aunt Mary so they could visit. I was holding on to what we considered normal as much as possible, but through this period, I learned to love and look at people differently. I had become a protector. Mama and Aunt Mary had become my charges. I would try to get anything they needed or wanted. For those people who touched our lives, I just wanted to be nice to them. However, the people, the relatives, that you would think would visit occasionally, did not, and those who maybe should not care actually paid attention. There was my ex-husband who went to the nursing home to see Aunt Mary once or twice a week. There was a young friend that Aunt Mary met at the nursing home who spent time with her. There was also a co-worker of mine who paid attention to what I was doing, and he helped me. Basically, no relatives really paid any attention. The bottom line is, within any given week, several people visited Aunt Mary. The nursing home did not really know when or who would show up and that was a blessing.

The nursing home arrangement went on for about three years. I learned a lot about life and love during that time. I learned how much Aunt Mary just loved people in general. She had a roommate, Mrs. Cheevey, who Aunt Mary tried her best to care for. If Mrs. Cheevey fell asleep uncovered, Aunt Mary would try to cover her so that she would not catch a cold.

One day, I found Aunt Mary crying. Her roommate told Aunt Mary that she smelled bad, and Aunt Mary cried. When this happened, I found that I could be the defensive back for Aunt Mary. This woman was a resident at the nursing home and out of respect for her age and condition, I had to figure out how to stop her from hurting dear Aunt Mary's feelings. So, I told her we all have odors sometimes. Sometimes I do, sometimes Aunt Mary might, and sometimes she may too. None of us like the conditions in which we find ourselves sometimes but we all must be just as kind as we can to each other and do the best we can. The woman had tears in her eyes when I finished talking to her. We never had that problem again.

I remember the time when a pipe burst at the nursing home, and I found out that Aunt Mary had been transferred to a nursing home on the other side of town about 40 miles away. At the new location, Aunt Mary's personality was so magnetic that the nurses hung out in her room or rolled her to the nursing station when she couldn't sleep in the middle of the night to stay with them. The nurses thought it was a perk for the residents to have a private room so for whatever reason they could conjure up, Aunt Mary would be assigned a private room. If there was a problem with Medicaid approving medicine that Aunt Mary needed, the nurses would tell me to go through the process and don't worry about it. The nurses told me if the medication Aunt Mary needed was in the building, she would get it on time.

During those days I was so mentally and physically exhausted, I just stopped acknowledging even being tired. It didn't matter anymore. I took comfort in balancing work with assisting two grand old ladies who had taken care of me impeccably. I settled into the idea that that was my life and that was what I did. I did have the assistance and kindness of many friends. On any given day, you could not tell who or when someone would volunteer to go see Aunt Mary on my behalf. There was a cute little girl named Misty who could have been Aunt Mary's granddaughter. Misty befriended Aunt Mary during her own rehab at the nursing home after a car wreck. There was a co-worker, Peter, who listened to me on the phone at work, trying to juggle a mean 9-5 job and do the best I could with the old ladies. There were the neighbors we had met after Mama and Aunt Mary moved in with me. There was my ex-husband, who really was a better friend than a husband. He helped as if we were still married or if he was their actual son. I always thank God for sending the angels who helped me to take care of the people who meant so much to me.

The next thing I learned is that even with all your patience, all your prayers, and all your efforts, nothing can change the progression of time.

One Sunday morning, a friend of Mama's, June, called from her high rise. She said that she could not get Mama to answer the phone. She said that they always talked about the same time each day. I spoke to Mama two or three times a day if I was unable to see her. I told June, "I'll be there in a minute." It took about 15 minutes for me to drive from my house to Mama's apartment. I remember there was jazz playing on the radio, and I was thinking *I hope she hasn't fallen.*

When I arrived at Mama's apartment door, I could hear the TV playing on the other side. I unlocked the door and saw that Mama was sitting on her couch with her head back. Her mouth was open, and her eyes were in a permanent glare. Mama was gone. I remember thinking, *it's alright, Mama, but it is not okay.* The conversations we had during the past few weeks became clear. She wondered where the relationships with my ex-husband and my family members were going. She told me where she thought I ought to live. She said that she had done all that she could. Now, thinking back on it, she was preparing to leave me all that time, but I refused and rejected the idea of really hearing the meaning of those conversations. As a matter of fact, one of her happiest days was when I had recently told her that I would miss her if anything happened to her because I really spent all of my free time either with her or talking to her. Boy, was that an understatement.

The major task at that point was to tell her sister, Aunt Mary, that Mama had died. Those two women had grown up together and then lived together, starting in their late 30's for 50 plus years. *Lord, have mercy.* During those last few years, I tried to become as close to being as strong for them as they had been for me. I had to be strong for Aunt Mary that day even though I was delivering bad news. I got into my car and drove to the nursing home on the north side of town to tell Aunt Mary. *Lord, have mercy.*

When I arrived at Aunt Mary's room, I put my arms around her and I said, "Aunt Mary, Mama is gone."

Aunt Mary scoffed. She looked at me and asked, "What do you mean?"

I replied, "Aunt Mary, Mama died last night."

Then, the two of us just sat and looked at each other with tears in our eyes. Something did not seem right. The set of three was now missing one of the pieces. There was nothing to say and there was nothing that we could do to put it back together. It was God's will. Like Mama used to say, "When God made the world, he got through with it. Period."

I liked having pictures of Mama everywhere, but Aunt Mary wanted pictures of Mama out of sight. She said that she could not bear to look at them. I tried to double up on the visits after Mama died. I had more time since I only had one location to visit at that point. In reality, I only had one close relative left, Aunt Mary. I tried to tell her how much I loved her and how much I needed her. She was 92 years old, and like Mama, she sat, even in her nursing home room, trying to tell me the best way to get things done in my life. They were smart women, so I listened.

The front of the nursing home was lined with benches, flowering trees, and plants. I would take Aunt Mary out to sit on the bench sometimes. She called that area the park. On one gorgeous day, the clouds were pink, and the breeze was light, and we just sat there together looking at the clouds. Then she uttered one of her characteristically kind statements to me.

Aunt Mary said, "I know that your Mama's death hurt you more than it hurt me. Since I came up here to live, I haven't seen her as much as you. I know it hurt you more."

That was her way of telling me that she knew that I was in pain, but I knew that she was in pain too. She had been with Mama all her life. The set of three had been broken, and yet it was a passage neither of us could escape.

A year later, Aunt Mary got an intestinal blockage, and she was just too old and fragile to survive that type of operation. *Lord, have mercy.*

The set of three was broken.

There were three, then two...

And finally, there was one.

I had two mothers who loved me and invested all that they had in making a decent life for me. In the end, it doesn't matter who loved you. The fact that you were loved and that you felt love makes the journey worthwhile.

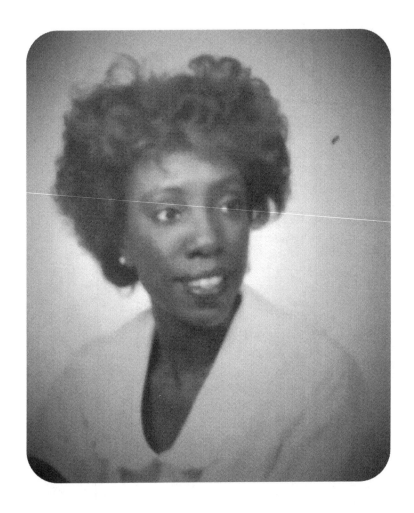

Debora Starr

LEARNING TO LOVE WHAT YOU HAVE

by Debora Starr

Rudy, Champion of chasing butterflies and sun reflections

It was late one morning in mid-spring, somewhere around 2010 or 2011. I was coming out of Costco. As I approached my truck, I could see a Clayton County Police car parked nearby. Considering that a police officer was examining my vehicle, I quickly had to surmise his business there. Oh yeah, I left Petunia in the truck. Within a few seconds, I analyzed the situation as I kept my pace and approached the patrol car.

The policeman spoke, "You don't have the windows down. I could not get into the car without breaking the window. You don't ever need to leave her in the car in this heat again. I already know who you are. You live in Stockbridge. It is just you and the dog that lives there. I know that you didn't mean to do the wrong thing, but what you did is not acceptable. I will let you go this time. Just don't do it again." He knew all of this about me and my dog. I did not even live in his county. Anyone who knows me knows that I take care of my dog very carefully. However, my lesson with this scenario is that leaving your dog in your car can get you locked up or fined.

Now, everyone in the free world knows that I would not do anything to hurt any animal—especially not Petunia. She was more like a roommate than my dog. We had gone on trips together. We survived being abandoned by just about everybody. We had gone through unimaginable circumstances together, and we were still hanging tough. As a matter of fact, the only reason she was in the truck is because I loved her, and she loved to ride shotgun. You should have seen her on long trips. I would stop to let her relieve herself and she would be like, "Get back in the car. Let's ride!" And, yes, she would be smiling while she said it. A song would come on the radio, and I would sing loud and out of tune while Petunia would sit, looking straight ahead, grinning. I realized that this was going to be one of her last long car rides before summer. It would be too hot for me to leave her in the car as the weeks progressed, but we could ride again starting in the fall. Sometimes we would go on overnight trips. Petunia was really my "road dog."

Anyway, I apologized to the policeman. And I said whatever it took to get him to go away so that we could be on our way.

I will always tell this story about Petunia. She was the dog who followed the dream dog, Daffodil, a beautiful classic Golden Retriever, with soft Golden Retriever ways, but Petunia looked soft and cute. Petunia was no joke. As a matter of fact, the inconsistency between her looks and her behavior made you laugh. Petunia was a foo-foo looking dog that would act like Cujo from time to time.

Petunia came to me with a bad attitude. When she was a puppy and I reached for the switch to tap her, Petunia reared back and barked. It was like an argument we were having. From that point, I had to learn to control her without being cruel and breaking her spirit. In reality, I had bought a dog that had dubious breeding, and she displayed a temperament that was a little strong for a poodle.

Petunia was well known on her block. She was a cute little Standard Poodle that was just too everything to be a standard anything. She barely grew large enough to be considered a Standard Poodle. She was almost too small to be a show standard. Her head and facial features were classically gorgeous. She had what you might call fear-aggression, but it was more than that. She was gutsy, bold, and very protective of me. No one would think that a poodle would act the way Petunia sometimes acted. As a matter of fact, it was her attitude which gave me pause when I first got her. I never wanted a dog that I had to prevent from hurting someone, but that was the attitude Petunia displayed. Later, I found out that Petunia really loved people and part of her barking, bouncing, and posturing was to get your attention. You had to meet her in order to know that.

One day when I arrived home, I saw blood in the garage. I quickly looked for Petunia and examined her. There was not one scratch on her, nor was there any blood. That told me that whatever it was that had come into Petunia's room, which was the garage, had to leave quickly and it took a little present from Petunia with them—more than a scratch.

If Petunia ever thought that I was in a position that might be compromising, Petunia would stand in front of me and bark to protect me. Even just a car coming into sight put her on high alert if I was anywhere around.

One night the doorbell rang at about 3:00 a.m. I woke up in a stupor, but Petunia was on point. She ran to the door and barked as if to ask, "Who are you? Why are you here? Who told you to come here?" As a matter of fact, she answered the door so efficiently I did not even have to think about it. I went back to sleep. However, Petunia and I made an agreement. From that point on, she would answer the door in her bold and bawdy manner to give me time to get ready to take care of whatever kind of business I needed to handle. Living together we had no fear. Everything was under control, and we knew our parts in the household operations.

I remember a repairman talking to her once saying, "You don't know this, but you are a poodle, and I am not going to let you intimidate me." That's right, Petunia was a "B-I-T-C-H," and she did her job well. If you ever spent the night with me, you would know that she patrolled the house. She slept by my bed part of the night and by your bed part of the night. However, by morning she would be back at my bedside.

Think about it. I could leave her in the car when the weather was right. No one was going to approach the car, and they damn sure were not going to steal her—not alive anyway. I could leave her in the yard. Standard Poodles can be a little pricey, and maybe someone would think to try and take one, but no one could approach the house without the whole neighborhood knowing about it. Petunia was small, but she was loud.

Petunia and I got into a rhythm. She was my roommate, and we perfected our routine. In her ninth year, Petunia was diagnosed with an incurable ailment. I braced myself for the journey and heartache. Have you ever received news that caused you to brace yourself for the mental anguish that is about to come? Well, I anticipated the bleakness of an empty spot in the house, so I got another dog to break the fall. Needless to say, Petunia was not crazy about the new addition. She did, however, tolerate him. The new dog stayed inside while I was away, but Petunia stayed outside with access to the garage. Petunia did not like being locked up inside the house.

One day, I set the alarm, and somehow the alarm went off while I was gone. Later that week, I saw a neighbor who approached me to ask if I was okay. He said that the alarm had gone off at my house, and the police had come. However, the police would not approach the house because Petunia raised such a ruckus that they knew no one could get past her while she was still on her feet. The police concluded that no one in their right mind would try to go by Petunia to go into the house. That is how Petunia took care of business and she was ill at that time—what a dog!

There are other stories I could tell about Petunia. What is important though is that she was always Petunia, quirky personality and all, until the day she had to leave. She never stopped protecting me and our house. As she became more ill, I put her in diapers. I changed her diapers and cleaned up her accidents while she tried to get to the door because she tried so hard not to have an accident. I got her an account at the drugstore and gave her medicine on time every day.

There was a cooperative community in my neighborhood, pulling for Petunia, but we all knew what the outcome would be. The community really was pulling for me though. People were coming out of the woodwork to help soften the blow. The only constant in this world is change. At that point, the change was that her little body just got too sick to go any further. I was blessed to have had her for 10 years.

The pain of giving her up was unimaginable. Your dog is your faithful friend when everyone has left, and everything has gone wrong. Think about this:

If you ain't cute, the dog doesn't care.

If you lose your job, the dog doesn't care.

If you ain't dressed right, it's okay with the dog.

If you sleep in the best place, just give the dog a place to sleep.

If you eat good food, just give the dog something to eat.

If you are cold, the dog might try to keep you warm.

If everything is lovely, the dog helps you celebrate and doesn't get envious

Petunia's special trait was guarding her master

Whatever goes wrong, the dog is there to go through it with you.

The dog just looks at you and in its own way says to you, "I'm with you, friend."

Losing Petunia made me wonder if the bad stuff that happens in this world is just a bad dream and the good stuff is a glimpse of happier reality. I hope so because I cannot imagine going to heaven and not feeling the kind of complete unquestionable love that God let me experience with my Petunia. In order to help me put my loss into perspective, the vet said to me, "Can you imagine a person who has not experienced the kind of relationship that you had with her?"

Always give thanks for what you have had.

PRETTY PACKAGES CAN HAVE EVIL CONTENTS

by Debora Starr

Have you ever heard that the mind tries to block experiences that are too painful to remember? Well, keep that thought in mind as I tell you about an experience that I should have forgotten, but it will always be just below the surface because it was such a hard lesson to learn.

It was not long after I bought my first house. I was a single woman in the city where I was born. I was young and in my late 20's. I dated men some but other than the occasional date and male friends, which did not last long for one reason or another, I was the woman who just worked and went to school. I guess you could say that I was progressive in the way that a woman reaching maturity during the early 1970's would be. I had a decent job, my own car, my own house, and I paid my own bills, but I was not street smart. Now don't get me wrong, I did enjoy the company of men like any other woman my age would. However, I was too busy going to school and working to recognize the danger in disguise. I did not have enough sense to proceed with caution, do research, and all the other clichés which are just a warning for a person to be careful.

My neighbor to the right of me was not speaking to me at the time. They seemed to be wary of me, the young, single black female that had just moved in next door to them. I guess they just did not know what to expect. But, on the other side of me, a young single black man moved in. *Yeah!* I remember peeking through my window while all his good-looking friends helped him move in.

My neighbor was friendly enough. He was single and a schoolteacher. He moonlighted on the weekend at a restaurant. We did not interact much. I worked nights, weekends, and any time my employer said, "Get here!" It was hard for me to meet or get to know anyone, and with my odd, undesirable schedule, it was hard for anyone to get to know me. My single male next-door neighbor was pleasant from a distance. He was relatively quiet even when his beautiful male friends visited. He rolled my garbage can up from the street every week and we had nice "weather conversations" when we talked to each other. We were friendly enough to share information about handymen or yard men, and that is how I met his friend Joe.

My yard needed cutting, but I was the type to cut my own yard. I really didn't mind cutting grass, even now I don't mind. However, every time I cut the yard, I got sick. I am highly allergic to grass, so when I found myself without a yard man, my neighbor suggested a friend of his to cut the grass.

Joe came to handle my yardwork and I paid him. He was pleasant and did a decent job. I gave him his money and he was gone. It was a simple transaction. The next time the grass was cut we were a little friendlier and I noticed something. This man was smooth, well-spoken, and drop-dead gorgeous. Now if you put all of that with a young woman who is not dating and is not likely to have any dates because of her schedule, this man just might be interesting. When he asked me out, I said, *yes.*

LESSON 1. GO SLOW AND PROCEED WITH CAUTION.

I found out that Joe was a construction worker. He was helping to build the new Marriott Marquis. He was from San Diego, California. We went out on our first date. I don't even remember where we went, but you must know that I was a young woman with a sheltered existence up to that point so a man with a racy and fast personality would have scared me enough to run. Let's just say that wherever we went and whatever we did, Joe's behavior was not aggressive or slick. I was too conservative to enjoy that type of date. However, it was known that he did drink socially. He did not do drugs. At that time, that was a major check point for me. I would barely drink an alcoholic beverage, but a person who had a drug habit has always been a problem for me. I would barely look at a person who did drugs of any kind. Let's not even talk about dating drug users. Joe did not use any drugs that my inexperienced eyes could determine. My neighbor knew him. He had a job. He seemed intelligent, he was a smooth conversationalist, and he was very good-looking. I enjoyed being with him, but I was not on the hunt for a husband at the time, so my analysis of this date did not go very deep.

LESSON 2. DO YOUR RESEARCH. CONFIRM
YOUR RESEARCH.

Joe and I met in late summer, and we had fun in the fall going to the local fairs. We were just hanging out. It was not unusual for me to take a date to my mother's house. My family was tight knit so if anyone was with me often enough, it would be easy for them to find themselves at Mama's house—even for just a minute.

I remember how easy it was for me to be with Joe. You know how you can meet a person and their presence is like something that you are accustomed to already? One day I said something sassy to him. That was normal behavior for me at the time. I was never a physical fighter, but I always answered with some form of an argumentative statement. Remember, I said that I was naïve. Now I know that sometimes it is better not to answer. It is better to just shut up, listen, back up, turn, and run, but I didn't know that at the time.

You know, a lot of times, you don't even remember what an argument is about. Well, my first encounter with Joe in an argument is one of those times when I can't remember the reason for the disagreement. Honestly, it was inconsequential. I just knew that I went to walk past him, and I ended up on the floor with his arm against my neck cutting off the air. I need you to understand that he did not hit me to get me on the floor. He tripped me and maneuvered in some way that I did not fall hard on the floor, but he made up for that by choking me, and all of this was done in a split second. It was like one continuous move.

When Joe took me down like that, I think he muttered something like, "Who are you talking to?" Of course, I could not answer and a second later he released me so that I could breathe again. No man had ever put their hands on me to hurt me so when I got myself up off the floor, I was in shock. Joe immediately grabbed me and apologized. He said, "I am so sorry," but I just looked at him. I did not know what to say. I am sure that I did not accept his apology. I was shocked—too shocked to even speak. I was so stunned and trying hard to understand what had just happened. He left.

I did not hear from him for about a week. Just as I began to wonder about him, I came home to see my grass cut. He appeared at my door within a couple of hours. When I opened the door, he stepped in and passionately apologized and kissed me. He told me how sorry he was for what he had done. Women who have been through this know that the right response was to not open the door, get the gun, and call the police. Me being naïve, a woman in love, lust, or whatever you want to call it, I allowed him to come into the house. I accepted his apology, and all was forgiven.

LESSON 3. IF YOU DON'T LIKE BEING BATTERED, LEAVE.

Let's just say a woman who is in an abusive situation does not forget that her abuser is subject to snap at any moment. When you have become a part of the syndrome you automatically go into a state of trying not to do anything to provoke him. You walk on eggshells. The problem is that you don't know what is going to set him off, and once you really analyze the problem, you know that it is not the provocation that causes violence. The problem is you should have stopped the S.O.B. dead in his tracks the first time he touched you. You need to let him know that you are crazier than he is and that you will hurt him or maybe worse. But if you are green to this type of situation, you end up just setting a trap for yourself by forgiving and continuing the relationship.

Anyway, nothing of any significance happened for a while. Then, my cousin and her date went to an arts festival with us. It was in the park during the fall. I was aware Joe had been drinking. His behavior was just a little different and not in a good way. We rode the city transit to avoid traffic and parking problems. Have you ever been with a person who has had too much to drink, and you try to ignore them, but the more you ignore them, the more obnoxious they get? Well, that was Joe's behavior that day.

On the way back home, while we were standing on the platform waiting for the train, Joe got really loud and I said something like, "Why are you acting like this? Don't do that." He responded, "Who are you talking to? Don't you know that I will throw you over on these tracks?" He must have made quite a scene because someone called the transit police. When he saw the police, he left me with my cousin and her date. I thought he was gone for the night. However, when we got back to my house, I found that my phone lines had been cut and my lights were disconnected. I locked the door and we got ready to leave the house just to be on the safe side.

We were getting into my cousin's car when Joe appeared on my front lawn. He grabbed me, threw me on the ground, and I could hear my cousin and her date in the background screaming, "Please go away. Don't act like this. Just go on." I managed to get away from him and I got into their car. We drove off, but he was racing along beside us on his motorcycle. I remember a male co-worker telling me to be careful because I worked at night and if anyone ever followed me, lead them to the nearest police station. So that is what we did. When Joe realized where we were leading him, he peeled off.

We went to the police station but were told that I could not file a report or complaint until Monday. We did not see

Joe anymore that night. We slept in a hotel. However, the police did come and investigate my house and they said what Joe did was even dangerous to him. He could have been electrocuted the way he cut the wires to the house. I believe he knew what he was doing though and how to do it. You will understand why I say that a little later.

Incidentally, it was after that episode my neighbor hinted that I might want to reconsider getting involved with Joe. I did ask him what he meant by that, but he just repeated what he said. I remember thinking, *why would anyone recommend Jack the Ripper to cut my yard if they already knew he was a shady character?* I did go to court, and I hired someone to go with me as a guard. I do know that Joe did not go to jail. I don't know how the law treats these types of situations now, but back then it was no big deal. Prior to my own troubles I remember hearing stories about couples where the man would beat the woman on the weekend, and it was considered neighborhood gossip—just something to talk about.

In the meantime, I was planning to move into another house. I had probably ridden by the house with him prior to the closing date before he revealed who he really was. I knew that he had arranged for a moving company to move me. That was already set up. However, continuing to date him was out of the question. I moved, and as far as I was concerned, that was a closed chapter.

LESSON 4. PREPARE YOURSELF FOR BATTLE.

I had not heard from Joe for several months. I had a double garage with double doors. I remember I had only one garage door opener, so I chained and locked one of the doors. One night when I got home, I remember finding the locks and chains inside of the house. Then he started calling. Once again, I cannot remember what the conversations were about, but I can tell you they were not friendly. They were eerie, threatening, and strange. I do remember him saying that he would watch me at night when I got off work and he would tell me what I had been wearing. And, yes, it was him that had come in and cut the chains off the garage door.

I was working the midnight shift. One day, I looked out of the window at the parking lot where my car was parked, and it wasn't there anymore. There were no cell phones back then, but I called his home, and he answered. I advised him that I had called the police and reported my car to be stolen.

Joe replied, "How can it be stolen when I have a key?"

While we were dating, he had access to my house and car. I did not know that he had a key made to my car. I told him that the police said that after a certain number of hours a car would be considered stolen, even if the person had a key, if it had been taken without permission. The next morning when I left work and headed to the parking lot, my car was where I had left it.

My co-workers knew that something was going on and I was in the right place. One co-worker insisted that I talk to the Battered Women's Organization. Two other co-workers insisted that I get a gun, and they taught me to shoot. Another co-worker called every night when I got off the second shift if I had not called him within 45 minutes of leaving the building. A co-worker was always circling around in his Jeep in the parking lot to make certain that I got into my car. My co-worker, Henry, arranged for me to go upstairs and talk to Sally, another woman who worked the third shift. Sally showed me her purse, which had a compartment for a concealed weapon. Although, it was against company policy to bring a weapon onto the premises, all the co-workers who worked the third shift knew who was carrying a weapon. The company would not assist you by allowing you to enter the building in a safer way, but everyone knew who could start shooting if they had to handle a domestic problem.

The Battered Women's Group can educate you in a few minutes if you listen. First, they tell you about the Honeymoon Period in the battered women syndrome. That is, you get beat up, beat down, treated badly, and belittled. Then the batterer comes back and does something wonderful to get you to put your guard down again. The next thing is batterers like to isolate you from your support group, whoever they are, so they have more control. The next thing the Battered Women's Organization tells you is to file a police report and report any and everything to the police to establish a record. I was told to call them even if I was just afraid to go into my house. Another thing they tell you is that if you have a gun and feel like you need to pull it out, you had better use it. Otherwise, you are a dead woman!

We never dated again. He would disappear for a couple of months and then he would call. Maybe he would say something about what I wore at work. I was afraid, but I, little quiet, naïve Debora, was packing. I slept with a gun under my pillow, but I was embarrassed about it. It broke my heart that I had to tell my family, but I could not possibly expose them to danger. I did not know Mama was packing too.

LESSON 5. ONCE YOU ARE IN THIS SITUATIION YOU MIGHT BE KILLED. ACCEPT IT AND PROCEED ACCORDINGLY.

During this time, I had a sick uncle in another city. He was the uncle that everyone said if he was well, he would come to Atlanta and take care of business. He would not allow Joe to terrorize anyone in his family, but Uncle Rich had a serious illness and could not come. Mama said he always asked what was happening with me though. She said that she did not want to worry about Uncle Rich, so she did not discuss it with him that much. Somehow, he still knew.

During this period, I had a dream about Uncle Rich. In the dream, he (who had never been to my house) was in the house. Uncle Rich walked around, looking, and said this is nice, but there is someone else in here that I can't catch up with. That was the end of the dream. What eventually happened occurred in the area of the house in the dream.

I lived on a hill that every house in close proximity could easily see. It was summer and the weather was hot. I had a habit of leaving the windows on the top floor open. Who would have thought that somehow Joe would climb into a window on the second floor, but he did. He disarmed the alarm system, and he was waiting on me when I went to turn the alarm off.

Joe put his forearm against my throat and said, "Don't scream."

We went down a couple of stairs to sit in the den. He sat on a chair, and I sat on the couch facing him. I had a gun under the pillow. It was a very quiet suburban neighborhood but, occasionally, you could hear a siren in the far-off background.

Joe looked at me and said, "Don't try anything slick. I am not going out of here with the police alive."

We did not talk much. I prayed—or at least I tried to pray—I said the 23rd Psalm. I asked Joe why he would hurt me when I had always been nice to him. I cannot remember the answer and it does not matter because in these situations, no answer is sufficient. There is no way to rationalize battering and terrorizing another person. After about an hour I begged him to allow me to call my mom. He said, *no.* I said if they do not get a phone call, they will send the police, because they will think something is wrong. Finally, he agreed, and I made the call.

My aunt answered the phone. In my state of confusion and fear, I said something that should have set off an alarm to her. I asked her about the condition of an uncle who had been dead for about two years. She said Quint is dead, and after a few other pleasantries, we hung up. She did not get that something was wrong. The police did not come and most likely if the police had come, I would have been dead.

I guess it was not my time to go. The next morning, Joe was ready to leave. He said, "I will leave you tied-up in the garage or put you in a remote location."

I begged him not to but instead he robbed me. He took my gun and took me to an ATM. He forced me to make a withdrawal. When he finally got out of my car, I drove straight to the police station and reported the incident. Detective Hammer said that they would charge him with kidnapping, battery, assault, and robbery, but they had to catch him first.

I guess I considered it good to work nights, although working late always gave me problems. But if I could not sleep at night because I was afraid, I might as well be working. Maybe he would not be as bold about pursuing me during the day hours.

Terrorized—that's what I was. I slept with a gun. Sometimes I slept at a friend's house who Joe did not know. Strangely enough, I grew close to her. We had something in common. She came to me previously for help when she showed up at work several times with a black eye. She would not go home. What is even stranger is that I did not remember how outraged I was that a man had driven her from her apartment where she paid the rent so she could stay with me. I could not remember how to get mad enough to break the chains in my own situation.

The next several months were the same. Joe stopped breaking into the house, but he would call me every other month it seems. He wanted to let me know that he had watched me in the parking lot at work. I remained crazy with fear for my safety, but I was even more afraid for my family. I would rather die than have them get hurt because I got involved with this horrible monster. The thought of them getting hurt was enough for me to swear that I would kill him.

Sometimes my mother or aunt would go home with me so that I could sleep in my own bed during the day. I remember being so tired from working nights and being on guard when I wasn't at work. One time Aunt Mary was at my house puttering around. She loved to wander around my house and fix things up for me. I was upstairs asleep, and she was tinkering around. I actually fell into a deep sleep in the middle of the afternoon so when I awoke from hearing something downstairs, I got my gun from under my pillow. I slid around the corner with the lever cocked and just before I pulled the trigger, I saw Aunt Mary. My stomach still turns over just with me thinking that I could have shot the love of my life. I don't think she ever realized what had happened.

It had been a year since he held me hostage in my house and it was again late summer when I got a call from

81

Detective Hammer, who said that they had got a hit on Joe. He had pawned the gun that he had stolen from me. Hammer said that somehow, they were going to get him and to just be careful.

Holidays, birthdays, weeks, and months meant nothing because I was always tense. When I thought that he had gone away, I would get a telephone call. But I did not see him again. However, he would call just often enough to keep the fear alive.

During that time, the most encouraging advice I got was to arrange to see him and then kill him. If I could arrange all of that, I could tell the police where he was. But I did come to that conclusion. I was weary and tired of being afraid that I had gotten myself into a situation with a person that might kill me. However, for the first time in my life, I had to believe that given the opportunity if the choice came down to killing him or letting him live, I would have to kill him. I accepted that if we ever came face to face again it was going to be him or me.

It had been about a year and a half that this terror ruled my life, and a few days before Christmas, I got another call from Detective Hammer. He said, "They got him." Joe was stopped on I-20 East and the car he was driving had broken down. The police spotted his fake out of state driver's license. Hammer said he was on the way to Covington to get him, but the police from Los Angeles were already on a flight to Atlanta to get him. He had murdered someone in California. Hammer said that we can get him back over here after California gets through with him, but he will have to serve his time in California. It was a few days before Christmas. *Merry Christmas to me!*

So, do you want to know what I learned? In order to make myself clear, I have been known to make the revealing statement, "I don't fight." While I am saying that, I don't smile, I don't blink, and I don't raise my voice. Long story short, I don't accept any type of threatening posturing, whether it is physical, verbal, or emotional. This is not acceptable, even in a joking manner, and I leave the minute it starts. I learned the hard way that if you are in a stalking and battering situation, you might end up dying.

You may be set up to get killed or to kill somebody. But you must stand your ground, firmly, from the very beginning on what you will not take and what you will not accept. These situations could easily have deadly consequences.

FRIENDS AND LOVERS

by Debora Starr

Consider this: have you met the love of your life? Can you have more than one person who comes into your life who can be a good fit? Considering hindsight is more accurate than what we can see when we are up close, would you recognize that what you have is good and what you have is the best you are going to get?

The day was June 20th in the year 2017. The phone rang. It was a familiar voice. It was the voice of a person who had been my friend for the last thirty years. The voice was so familiar that there was no need for the caller to announce himself—he just started talking. It was the habit of this friend to talk in a very upbeat manner over the phone. In thirty years, I cannot remember him conversing over the phone in anything but a cheerful, sing-song kind of voice.

My friend said, "Hello, how are you doing?" He continued, "I am at home now. I am out of the hospital. Oh boy, I tell you, I am never going back to that place again." He chuckled. He said something else that I will always remember, and I will tell that to you later.

I replied, "Hi, how are you? I am glad you are feeling better. I know that it is hard for you to get your breath when you talk, so just let me talk."

I scrambled for something else to say. These were the days when there was nothing specifically important to talk about. The actual words we spoke were only part of the conversation. The important part of the conversation was just to hear the person's voice—just to hear the other person being able to speak was all that was important because you knew one of you would be dying soon.

About thirty years ago, I met a man at a bar while we were playing cards who would eventually become my husband. When I walked into the dimly lit room, another friend of mine introduced me to this group of people who routinely met there on Wednesday nights. During the previous year, I had been in a relationship that was so bad it left me shell shocked and uninterested in meeting new people, but eventually, I was persuaded to come out to play a game of cards that I loved so much.

Before I sat down, this guy, John, was a little too friendly and he kept trying to say something to me. I remember that as passes go, I was annoyed by his attempts to make conversation, and I found his antics silly and annoying. But, sometime during the night, I gave my telephone number to him. I am certain I took his number as a means of narrowing the odds that he was already attached to a woman. It did not matter, because I really did not like him much anyway.

All my life, I have been a woman who was a sucker for men with the *gift of gab*—smooth talkers who could hold a conversation and knew how to work it. These are the men who are talking to you, and it seems like just a normal conversation on some topic. In reality, these are the men who are so smooth that you do not notice at first or care in the end that you have just let your guard down to be pursued.

However, John did not have the gift of gab. As a matter of fact, I can't remember what we talked about that night, but I do know that I did not get substantive meaning out of the conversation. After we got to know each other better, we laughed about the times when I was talking about one thing and he was talking about something else, neither of which were related. We called those disconnected conversations "blue moon" conversations.

John did not waste a lot of time before he called me. I talked to him the very next day, but once again, I cannot remember what we talked about. He was persistent though. He called me the next day, and the next day, and the next day until I agreed to go somewhere with him.

That first date was to a park or a nearby resort for the day. Truthfully, I really cannot remember which one. What I do remember is that when we went out, I found that John was friendly, funny, and easy to be with. Being with him was neither exciting nor boring. It was just easy to be with him. This guy did not pull any punches. He was not overly aggressive, and he was not shy either. We went on a few dates and got a little bit more comfortable being together. We met in the spring and by late July I had asked him to go to Mom's house with me to celebrate Aunt Mary's 78th birthday. The celebration would be just the four of us. I did not expect that he would want to join me, but he did. That day was July 23 about thirty years ago.

Now the facts about John were as follows—he was born in New York. He is seven years older than me. His mother was born in Atlanta but moved to New York. Years later after talking, we realized that as a child, she lived on the same street that I did as a child. He had one brother who had worked for the New York Transit system. His brother had his first heart attack when he was in his early 40's. Evidently, heart disease ran in the family. His father died of cardiovascular disease when he was in his 50's. John had attended a specialized high school in New York which was heavy on mechanical training and light on academic training. He had joined the Army when he was eighteen and trained to be a helicopter mechanic. He got married for the first time when he was nineteen. He had two children during that marriage, but it ended when extramarital affairs led to a tragedy which I will not discuss here.

After getting divorced from his first wife, nine years later John married again, and that union brought one child. That marriage lasted a couple of years before it ended. Six years after his second divorce he met me, and I became wife number three after we dated for about two years. After he got out of the military, he studied to become an aircraft mechanic and worked for East-West. At the time I met him, East-West Airlines was tanking, and eventually went out of business. I prayed for East-West Airlines to die, so that my husband could go on with his life, but if you are an Atlantan, you probably heard some of the stories about how some of the people who worked for East-West never recovered. My husband never fully recovered either, but the two of us survived. We survived— sometimes in spite of each other.

How did we survive? I was a household budget conservative and still am. I don't care if I don't go on vacation. I don't care if I don't go on a cruise. Secondhand clothes don't bother me, and new clothes need to be on sale. There are not a lot of things that I don't like to eat but what I do like to eat cannot cost a fortune. My policy is if you dine out often, you do not need to buy a lot of groceries for the house. My freezer and cupboard are always full. I buy things on sale. It is just a family habit that I cannot shake. Oh yes, and if I cannot keep a car for ten years, then the car was a lemon.

My husband was not a clothes horse. He did not love cars, and I can honestly say that he was not a womanizer, but he did love his liquor and partying. He was the party animal, but I was not. He was the drinker, but I was not. So much for the birds of a feather flocking together thing.

After being married to John for two years, I divorced him. I did not like the fact that he was a functional alcoholic. I was afraid that he would get killed or kill someone driving drunk. I could not see him making any plans to go forward. Before we divorced, I shouted and screamed, and he answered. We never physically fought, but one night I had my gun under my pillow when he got home from driving his taxi. I had been through an abusive relationship prior to meeting him, and I just was not going to take any abuse. Funny thing is, he normally left his gun in his car, he brought his gun into the house that night. That could have ended badly.

The final straw was when one of John's ex-wives got me on the phone and told me what he was supposed to be doing for her and her child. I thought *he no longer has the big paycheck so if he can do anything for you at all, it is partially because of me. I am helping him.* It was after that telephone call, I made up my mind that I was divorcing all of them. I recall the film, *War of the Roses*, and I understand every part of it. In fact, the two of us watched the movie together with our mouths and eyes wide open. It was as if someone had filmed what went on in our house.

If you have ever been through a divorce, they are seldomly pleasant, and ours was no exception. There was as little ceremony divorcing John as there was when I married him. The day I divorced him, I got up from my desk and marched down the street to the courthouse. I went in, signed some kind of papers with a bunch of other people in the room who were doing the same thing, and then it was a done deal. If you have ever seen pictures of mass weddings—well, this was a mass divorce. I had left my desk unfinished, so I went back and finished my work for the day. A co-worker who knew me well, who I can still call a friend today, heard me crying, and came to my desk to comfort me. I told my coworker that I felt I had to divorce him to save myself, but I still loved him.

After that, one day I was angry, and I showed it in front of my mother. I will never forget what she told me. She said, "You need to be careful how you treat people. You never can tell who will have to turn you a favor." I do try to remember that message today since what she said was wise and prophetic.

My ex continued to visit my mother even though I had just divorced him. As a matter of fact, when we had arguments, a lot of times John ended up at Mama's house. Mama would mention sometimes that he had visited, but I would not tell her that we had an argument. I do not remember the exact period of time that we went without seeing each other—maybe for about six months—but I do know that we resumed within one year.

For the next twenty-plus years, John and I were exes, friends, and lovers. We were married, although legally we were divorced. That small technicality kept us together. We were around each other purely by choice. Neither of us dated anyone else or got involved with anyone else. You know a lot of times you cannot be certain what a man or a woman might do on the side. However, in our case I can be fairly certain because we were with each other so much and always available to each other on a weekly, daily, or hourly basis. There just was not enough time for either of us to really have someone else on the side.

I bought my first house when I was in my early twenties. By the time I met John, I was in my second house. I suppose he was impressed by whatever I did which came easily to me. I had established a time-tested way to handle a household—basically by stretching a dollar. Although, I am a jack of all trades and a master of none, I am a decent housekeeper, cook, seamstress, and gardener—heavy emphasis on the word *decent*. I was however impressed with his "just fix it" skills. Nothing in the house would be left unrepaired with John around. He was a plumber, an electrician, and a carpenter, and he could fix anything on a car. I would watch him make up ways to handle problems and it was like watching a person applying engineering principles to everyday problems. It took me a little while to figure out that he had a natural talent for fixing and making things, and he had gone to school basically all his life to learn the principles. Yet I was on the other end of the spectrum. I had always loved academia and nerdy subjects came easily to me.

I remember one time I was at Five Points in downtown Atlanta at the Gibraltar Bank. When I came out, my car started right up, and I left the parking lot. But once I was out in traffic, the car would barely move. I could not get up any speed. I called John to come and help me. I don't know what he did, but within 10 minutes, I was rolling again, and I was good. Thinking back, we were always available and ready to help each other. Anytime I called, he would be at my side within the hour. And, he could always count on me to have his back if he needed it.

I used to get slightly irritated when a repairman came to the house. My husband-lover-friend would watch him and talk to him about what he was doing. He knew enough principles and terminology across various mechanical subjects to engage in meaningful conversations with the repairman. It took me a while to understand that the repairman never had to come back to the house. My husband would always make the next required repair.

One time, John explained to me how he was able to understand fixing or making many different types of things.

"Remember, I went to a school where we had 15 minutes of English per week and 15 hours of shop," said John. "I was an aircraft mechanic, and airplanes have lots of different types of systems, so you have to know how they work and how to fix them."

Truthfully, he had a natural talent for dealing with mechanical issues. When I realized his unusual ability, I would just stand back and watch him calculate what to do. He would create solutions that worked and think nothing about it.

As far as skill sets go, we complimented each other well. On a social level, we were just as compatible together. We both liked playing cards, and we could entertain each other for hours. However, the fact remained that John was the drinker and partier, and I was the person with life management skills that would keep both of us afloat. At that point, we did not to try to control or change the strengths of each other anymore. He let me handle what I was good at doing, and I did not even look back when he was in his element handling problems.

With the many houses and cars I owned, John was there for me. He was there for me on holidays without fail. We lived together sometimes, and other times I could not take his abuse of alcohol and poor personal discipline skills, so we did not live together. All my friends and family loved and accepted him as the one that was always going to be with me. He had a friendly, unpretentious manner about him that people still speak of today.

John's family, with the exception of his mother, Viola, did not love me so much. I learned:

- Be careful who you vent to.
- Sometimes your people are not YOUR people.
- Watch the dynamics of a relationship. If they stay together voluntarily, they are getting something that they need.

90

- There are at least two sides to every story, and they are not the same version of what happened.
- Sometimes you have to be one of the parties involved to really understand how this works.
- Sometimes the parties don't even understand. They just know that it works.

John's mother, Viola, really liked me. I was surprised to find that out, because she did not spend a lot of time with me, and I wasn't shy about telling her what I thought about her son—good and bad.

To my complaints Viola answered, and to my surprise, "Well, he has known a lot of good women, and by this time I know that it can't always be the fault of the woman. Sometimes, it has to be his fault."

Just before she died, I found out that she truly did like me. Viola was sick, but when I walked into her hospital room, she lit up and told her male companion, "That's her." He replied, "That's the one that sends Bingo money to you?"

Viola sent a handmade spread to me just before she got really ill. She sent one to her granddaughter, one to the other son, and one to me. Now, I can look back on it and know that she was choosing a person who she knew would try to be good to her son and take care of him as a friend. She was a smart woman.

It was late in my relationship with John when I found out that his mother drank too much also. It would seem alcohol was a family affair—I just did not know how deep the problem was until after I married John. They were all functional alcoholics. They did not look like alcoholics, but their need to have alcohol around was ever present. It still pains me to this day to say that there was an alcohol problem in his family, but it's true.

My immediate family was small. It was Mama, Aunt Mary, John, and me—four people who were always there for each other. I remember when John's mother died in New York. When he was back in town after the funeral, he went over to my mother's house. He was disheveled. He could get like that sometimes. I assumed the duty of helping him to keep up his appearance. He was an attractive man. He was not vain about it in any way, but if things got hectic or hard for him, appearance was the first thing he took off his plate.

This time, when he went by Mama's apartment, she asked, "What's wrong with your hair, John? Do you want me to give you some money to get a haircut?"

John had married into a family that would assume responsibility for making certain that he always had somewhere to go and be sheltered, get food, and keep himself in decent order. On the other hand, the family of women had found a man that knew how to keep them in decent order, taking care of traditional male duties quickly and without a lot of fanfare. We all loved each other. We all complimented each other in our functionally dysfunctional family, and it could not have been more perfect for us.

As I try to tell this story, I can remember now when things began to fall apart, or maybe they just took a natural course to come to an end. I have a saying I crafted: *if you think you have got it going on, don't get cocky because that can and usually does change. If you think that everything is wrong, you need to just hold on because things can change, and they usually do.*

The only thing you can count on to remain constant is change. So, this is where things started to change for the end of the story to begin. I always wanted a new house. I mean brand new. I had starter houses and I had a couple of houses that I bought to accommodate Mama and Aunt Jeanie, but I never had a house that was brand new. Additionally, John and I had done some heavy moving and renovation projects together, of which my part involved being the logistics manager and helper. The engineering and implementation were John's part. So, when I found a house where we could start together, I bought it. My hope was, even though I was handling the financing, if he was with me when I started to see how I balanced and maneuvered, if he would join in rather than just being a support, that we would be on the way to being one helluva couple. I found a beautiful house, but my thought was to buy low and sell for small a profit, just before we retired.

John loved the house and was proud of it, but he just did not know how to make an investment so that he would be fully invested in the project. In other words, he was horrible with his finances, and it did not matter what the cost was of pulling this deal together, he maintained his minimum monthly contribution while I struggled with the rest. That's okay because that was truly the test. If we started out together with something, I wanted to know if he would take the lead sometimes. The answer was simply that he would not. He blew whatever money he had left after making his minimum contribution, and we argued and argued about it all—his drinking, his lack of assuming ownership, and his family interjecting negative influence into our relationship. Finally, one argument was so bad, he went and got himself an apartment and left me holding the bag in a situation where I desperately needed his minimum contribution.

However, God is good. You better believe that there is a higher power. Someone and something bigger and more powerful than our frail efforts exists out there. Within six months, a real estate agent who knew that I wanted to sell the house brought someone by to look at it. The house was not for sale, but this woman wanted to buy it to which I replied, "How soon do you need me to be out of here?"

John told me he did not want me to sell the house, but my experiment with his lack of responsibility was over. I was lucky enough to sell a house that I wanted to get rid of without it being on the market. I moved into a house in a location that I absolutely hated, and once again John helped me to move and made repairs. This place was good because it was near people that I knew, including him. Also, I bought it because it was convenient to get to other places, but I hated it with passion.

Although John and I did not live together at that point, his apartment was close by, and his job was even closer. He repeatedly told me that he wanted to move out of the apartment. He did not say that he wanted to move in with me again. Of course, I would have let him, but this time, I wanted him to come up with a plan as to how it would work. I honestly think that women get tired of permanently being the "force" in a relationship.

I was about three years from retirement and John's retirement was even closer. Mama and Aunt Jeanie had passed away. If John and I tried to make it work again, it would have been the first time that we would not be caregivers. However, he moved out of state, and he did not tell me he was moving. We were close and, considering that we were always together, we were also always apart. I understood why he did what he did. However, I immediately knew that his decision was one that would hurt both of us in the long run. He had little family and I essentially had none now. We knew each other better than anyone knew either of us.

I did not try to call John, but a month later he called me and told me that he had moved. I replied that I knew he had moved. I also knew the minute that I heard his voice that we still had an unbreakable bond—one that disagreements, divorce, and distance could not destroy.

For the next three or four years, John visited me often. He came to visit on his birthday and on mine. He would come prepared to fix everything in my house and take me and my single friends out dancing. I never found anyone who complimented my personality and needs as well as he did, even though he was long distance at that point. I suppose he did not either. He gave a key to me and laughingly told me how his family members had conjured up all kinds of ideas about him not having a lady friend.

That situation lasted for about six years when John began to call me to tell me that he was in the hospital or not feeling well. He was never a complainer, but he knew that I would come to him if I knew. It became apparent to me that we should clear the air. I would come to him anytime he wanted. Twice when I had surgery, John came to stay with me. However, I did tell him that he needed someone in the city where he lived, and I needed someone also. We did not talk about it anymore, but I loved him enough to set him free if needed. I am not certain about how he felt about me dating someone. I do know that we did not flaunt whatever we did.

John got sicker and sicker. It was fluid retention from a bad heart that made it hard for him to breathe, and he developed a spot on his lungs. A couple of times, I piled my dog and some clothes in the truck and went to see him for a couple of days. Sometimes I think that the character of a person is shown when they are going through tough times. Looking back, I know that what he lacked in personal management skills, he came out looking like a hero dealing with the hard times that he was having.

John rarely complained about money, but I knew that the amount of his retirement check made it hard for him to pay for a place to live and have food and transportation. When he would come to visit me, he took care of everything that was broken, and I would give him a little money—I had to pay someone anyway.

My John never said that he felt bad. He might describe what was going on—maybe—and then move on to the next subject. He made me laugh when he said he was sitting on the table in the doctor's office and the doctor told him that he had about six months to live. He said he looked at the doctor and looked around in the room, and then asked the doctor, "are you talking to me? I believe that I can beat that." We both laughed when he told that to me, and he did beat the odds by about three years.

I told John, after marrying him and divorcing him, that I wanted to be more than his wife or lover. I wanted to be "Leah." I wanted to be that space in his life that could be only satisfied and filled by one person. I don't know if he ever understood exactly what I meant, but I think I made it to that place.

One day John looked at me and said, "Sometimes I don't know whether you are more like a sister, a wife, or a lover. I just don't know."

You see, husbands can be replaced, and lovers can be replaced, but it is the friend that you can only identify by their name that is forever.

We were lovers. I wanted our definition of being a lover to transcend the normal physical aspect of the act. In my mind, animals go through the act of procreating, so that is no big deal. I used to tell him that he had met a woman that could love him and be a lover to him and not have to touch him or be touched. Sometimes it is hard for a man to understand that concept, but once again I think John was able to get to that place.

Once when I went to visit John, he gave up his bed so that I could sleep in the room where he had complete bedroom accommodations. We did not touch or look at each other in any type of sexual manner. He was too sick for that, and the purpose of my visit was to be with him and help him for a few days. We both knew without talking about the subject that anything outside of pure love and friendship would have perverted the purpose of our time together, but when I got back home, he said one of the sexiest statements I have ever heard a man say.

"I can still see you laying across my bed," said John. "I guess I should stop seeing you and saying that with my sick self."

I couldn't help but smile. John's remark took my memory in two directions. One direction was when the chemistry between us was explosive, and the other was the fact that early on I knew that I could love him without the physical aspect.

Time progressed and John got sicker. He physically and mentally gave up his tools. He loved tools. He loved tools like women love shoes. I should have made a mental note of what was happening because this was an important turn of events, but once again, I did not want to see it.

John's feet and legs swelled. He was on oxygen because he could not breathe on his own. His daughter, who often butted into our business, only went to visit him about three or four times a year. John's brother passed away. Even in his condition, John caught a flight alone to New York and got into a cab to go to his brother's funeral. He had such a positive and determined spirit. I will try to remember his determination and take that as a lesson for myself as I age and get weaker.

Fast-forward to early June 2017. John and I did not have a schedule to talk over the phone. There was an internal clock for both of us which said *you need to call now*. We had discussed that if either of us called and left no message everything was okay. But without discussing it, we knew that we should talk within the next couple of days calling just to stay in touch and say everything was okay. Well, I made the call, and I did not get an answer. He did not return the call the next day or the next day or the next one.

My mind said *okay, something is wrong.* I just happened to have John's son's phone number. When I called, he advised me that his dad was in hospice care at the hospital. I called John to talk to him. He just laughed and said that he was "still kicking but not very high." I did not call him again while he was in the hospital. He got out of breath easily. He was in the best place he could be considering the circumstances. His son told me that they were trying to decide which way to go after that episode because he could no longer live alone.

About two weeks later, John called me. His voice was strong and upbeat. Remember this was still June 2017.

The last thing he said to me was, "I dreamed that I went to sleep and when I woke up you were here".

I heard him. This man, who did not have the gift of gab, every once in a while, could say things with meanings that touched so many areas that what he said would stay with you forever.

I dreamed that I went to sleep and when I woke up you were here. The statement is sexy without being sexy. It is loving without using the word love. It gave me a place of importance in his life without him having to say, *"You are important to me."* And it told me that he wanted me there without him saying, "Come to me now."

About three weeks later, John died. When he was lying on his death bed, I could not go be with him. He once said to me about my mother's death, "You can barely hold yourself together with you not being there when she died. What would you have done if you were standing there and could not do anything to stop it?" I realized that he was right on that occasion, and he would understand me not coming to him then.

John died on July 23, 2017. For some reason, after he died, the song *What Are You Doing the Rest of Your Life* reminded me of him. If there is a connection between life and death, I choose to believe that it is him telling me that he will be with me for the rest of my life. I will always remember my husband and lover who had the most important role of being my forever friend.

Finally, consider this: You may not know love when you first see it, but if you experience it, you can sense the essence of it if it ever happens again.

MY MOM'S MEDICINE AND OTHER MEDICAL STORIES

By Doris Thomas

*Stories about Mama's battle to keep us
healthy, growing up in a segregated
metropolitan area of the South, and growing
up in Atlanta.*

When I was growing up, my mother did not take me and my brother to the local hospital because she believed the doctors were members of the Ku Klux Klan and did experiments on negroes. Instead, she treated us with herbs she purchased from the curb market on Edgewood Avenue, or she went back home to Milstead, Alabama to get herbs from Ma Mandy. I only remembered her going to Grady Hospital once when she severely cut her wrist while trying to break a window after locking herself out of the house. She was given penicillin and had a severe allergic reaction. She was unable to work for over a month—not due to the injury—but due to the allergic reaction to the medication. My brother and I were never taken to the hospital. But later, when Dr. A.M. Davis, a negro medical doctor opened a practice on Auburn Ave. in Atlanta, my mom took us to him. When my mom became ill with a lung disease, Dr. Davis made house calls to see her. He was also the president of the NAACP and an activist.

At that time there were two hospitals for Negroes in the Atlanta area owned by Black doctors—McLendon Hospital and William Harris Memorial Hospital. They were located near or on Hunter Street, which is now Martin Luther King, Jr. Drive. However, both hospitals had limited space leaving the only other option of the Colored Grady Memorial Hospital for negroes. I only remember my mother taking me to Grady one time when my Aunt Mildred took me to the Atlanta City Auditorium for a gospel concert with Shirley Caesar, the Soul Stirrers and other top gospel singers. I was about thirteen or fourteen years old.

After Aunt Mildred and I left the auditorium, we went to Henry's Grill on Auburn Ave. a short distance from the auditorium. I had shrimp for the first time. When I arrived home a friend wanted me to go to the Royal Theater on Auburn Ave. to see *Man with the Golden Arm*, starring Frank Sinatra. While there, I went to use the restroom during the show. There was heavy cigarette smoke in the restroom. I started to have difficulty breathing after leaving, and I thought the cigarette smoke caused me to have an asthma attack. I had to take a taxi home because I was having such a hard time breathing.

When I got home, my mom called a taxicab and took me to the Colored Grady Memorial Emergency Room. The doctor examined me and informed me that I had severe asthma and an allergic reaction to the shrimp I had eaten and there was nothing he could do for me. I was placed in the hallway without further treatment. My mother picked me up and ran her fingers down my throat causing me to vomit. I started to breathe better and was sent home. Once home, my mother started to mix herbs for me to take. I was home for a couple of days, but I recovered without western medicine.

Before this episode, Mom always gave us herbs for any illnesses or infirmities. For chest congestion, we were rubbed down with tallow, a hard-fatty substance that can be melted. Tallow was also used to make soap. Mom smeared it on our chest and covered it up with a warm, flannel cloth to help open our lungs. Sometimes Mom would give us half a teaspoon of Vicks Salve to take along with some warm water. When she put us to bed, she placed a hot plate beside us on a chair with a boiler on top of it. She would put Vicks Salve in the water, and when it started to boil, steam would rise with the Vicks Salve permeating the room and loosening the congestion in our lungs. Sometimes Mom would use a white sheet to create a tent over the twin bed to keep the steam in so it would work faster on the chest congestion.

During the fall we were given several herbs to prevent illness. Some of the herbs were yellow roots, a very bitter tasting herb that my mom said would clean our system. A cough suppressant, called 666, was given to us to cleanse our system. It was also used for colds. Another remedy given to us was Black Draught powder or syrup. The main ingredient in Black Draught was senna leaf, a stimulant to cause bowel movement. Black Draught was given to us three or four times a year, mostly during the winter months. Sassafras tea was also given for inflammation when we were very ill. She gave us castor oil in our Coca Cola. I still don't care for Coca Cola because of the association with castor oil. We were also given a drop of turpentine on sugar to prevent worms and other parasites.

Both my brother and I suffered from asthma, but my mom refused to take us to the segregated hospital for treatment. For asthma attacks she always gave us herbs. SSS Tonic was given for iron deficiency. Sometimes in the fall and winter, she would make us a hot toddy using gin, honey, and rock candy. A teaspoon was given for congestion.

I remember when I was in about the fourth grade, I started having asthma attacks at school. When the first one happened, I thought it would go away, but by the time I arrived home, I was very sick. My mother gave me herbs and rubbed my chest down with tallow. I was having severe chills. Our home was heated with wood burning stoves and a fireplace in the middle room. To keep me warm, my mom put chairs in front of the fireplace and placed the twin mattress on them, so I was able to lie on the mattress in front of the fireplace to get warm.

When I was in the eighth grade, I came down with a cold and fever. I was not able to sleep well because of the coughing, and I didn't feel like going to school. My mother and her cousin thought I was "putting on," and decided to hold me down, pinch my nose, and pour castor oil down my throat. When I didn't recover as fast as she thought I should, she took me to see Dr. Davis, who told her I had pneumonia and the castor oil and other treatments she gave me saved my life. He gave me penicillin and cough medicine, but my mom continued to give me her prescribed herbs.

I did start to use the clinics at the hospital when I got married because I thought modern medicine would be better. However, I learned that it was not always better. I also used Dr. Davis, who was still very good. I learned that the American Medical Association—the white medical association—would not allow Negro doctors to join, which kept them out of the loop on new information regarding medicines. However, negro doctors formed their own association to assist one another.

The other time I remembered my mom using Grady Hospital was when my baby cousin became ill. I guess my mom had done all that she could do to get her well, and then decided to take her to the clinic. The doctor said that my cousin should be placed in the hospital. This occurred in the summer months, so I was out of school. My mom said I had not given my cousin the herbs I should have, so I was responsible for my cousin's illness. As a result, I was delegated to walk to Grady two times a day—breakfast and lunch—to feed my cousin, and I always waited for her to fall asleep before I headed home. My mom would go by the hospital after work to feed her and stay with her. I remembered the large pediatric ward with lots of steel baby cribs. Every time I entered the ward, she would be standing up looking through the crib bars, crying like she was in jail. She was always happy to see me.

I was a tomboy growing up. I loved to play baseball and football. The adults and children in the neighborhood would play baseball in a large field behind the houses. The adults would choose the children they wanted on their teams. I remember a lot of yelling, screaming and laughing during those baseball games. I especially loved football. The boys didn't treat me like a girl when we played. Consequently, while I was playing football I was tackled. Oh, did I mention the game was played on the street?

While playing, my left breast hit the curb causing a great deal of pain. My breast was left black and blue. When I finally went to the Colored clinic, I was informed that my breast would have to be removed. I was 14 at the time. My mom and I agreed that was not a good idea. I had surgery about 40 years later to remove a cyst. The breast is still holding, but it is a bit saggy.

After the birth of my fourth child, I went back to the OB-GYN clinic for my six-week checkup. The doctor looked at my upper left arm and saw a mole that he said was not there before. He asked me how long it had been there, and I told him I had not noticed it. He left the room and I heard him out in the hallway talking with another doctor about my arm. The doctor said that he thought I had melanoma. It so happened that I spent a lot of time lying in the sun and sometimes fell asleep. The doctor decided to refer me to the surgery clinic for follow-up.

The doctors at the surgery clinic decided that surgery was necessary because the mole was growing so fast. Melanoma is a form of cancer that grows rapidly. I left the hospital and did not return. The hospital eventually contacted my mom and informed her about my arm. She was able to convince me that I should have the surgery.

When I awoke from the surgery, my left arm was swaddled in bandages, and I could not move it. I wasn't sure if I still had an arm. The doctor came in to inform me that the surgery had gone well, and he was happy he didn't have to amputate my arm. I told him that no one had ever informed me they might have to amputate my arm. He told me that when I signed the consent form, it allowed them to do whatever they deemed necessary. I told the doctor if he had amputated my arm, I would have had some corner boys beat him up. He told the nurse to give me something to put me to sleep because I was talking out of my head, but I was not. I was angry because the doctor had not fully informed me of the type of surgery he might have to do.

The doctor removed so much muscle tissue from my arm they had to use barbwire to pull the skin together. I was so embarrassed by the scar left by the surgery I would not wear short sleeves after. One time I wore a short sleeve blouse, and someone asked me what happened to my arm. I told them my husband had caught me with my boyfriend and cut my arm. They were shocked, but I thought it was hilarious. It was years before I had the courage to wear short sleeves again. Since I stay cold most of the time, I don't wear short sleeves often anyway.

My other negative medical experience at the hospital came when I was experiencing heavy bleeding and pain. I went to the clinic and was told that they needed to do a test. While the doctor was examining me, I felt severe pains but thought it was all in my mind. When he was finished, I looked down and saw he had a baby food jar full of bloody tissue. I told him I thought the pain was in my mind. He told me that it was because I couldn't feel pain in my uterus. I told him if I couldn't feel pain in my uterus then let's use the scalpel and do the same thing to his penis. He told me that I could have cancer. I told him I would not be returning because he might try to remove my uterus without anesthesia. I did not return even though he said I had abnormal cells.

I found out later that the doctor had performed a dilation and curettage (D & C). During this brief surgical procedure, the cervix is dilated, and a special instrument is used to scrape the uterine lining. D & Cs are still done under general anesthesia.

The last but not the end of the stories I could tell at this time is of a colonoscopy in the hospital. My father died from cancer. Because I was experiencing some of the same symptoms, it was decided that I needed to have a colonoscopy. A colonoscopy is a procedure in which a flexible tube type instrument is inserted through the rectum in order to examine the colon or rectum. When I had the first colonoscopy at the hospital, I was placed on a table, straps were placed on my wrists, and a wide strap was put across my mid-section. The tube was inserted into my rectum. The pain was off the charts, especially when the tube reached a certain area of the colon. I was later told that area was "kicked off," so it was difficult to pass the tube beyond that point.

A few years later I had the same procedure performed by a private physician with the use of anesthesia. When the tube reached the same area again, I came out of the sleep because of the pain. I could hear the doctor telling the person responsible for administering the anesthesia, "She is coming out, put her under." I was only awake for a second. The doctor told me how I had come up fighting. I sometimes wonder how I was able to withstand the pain of the first colonoscopy.

These events occurred during segregation when equal treatment for Blacks was not always available. The black side of the hospital was often overcrowded while the white side had empty beds. Someone asked me how I felt about the hospital. My response was that as soon as there were hospitals that allowed Black doctors to admit patients, I would start using them. I always used Black doctors, but they did not always have access to hospitals. This was not because they were bad doctors. It was because they were discriminated against.

As a result of my many medical experiences, I have come full circle and now have gone back to my mother's roots by using herbs. A few years ago, an OB-GYN doctor suggested that I see a naturopathic doctor for health problems I was having. I visited the naturopathic and she said she could help me. Everything she said I needed to do, I told her my mom had done the same when I was young. She finally said to me, "Isn't it something that you are now paying a white female to do what your mother taught you to do for yourself?"

MOONSHINE STORY #1

by Doris Thomas

*This is the story of the bootlegger next door,
trying to stash illegal liquor under our house.
He was unable to hide his whiskey under our
house because our dog, a chow, would begin
to bark whenever he or his worker tried to
get under there.*

We lived next door to the community's bootlegger. Our
houses rested atop red brick columns, making it possible to
crawl under them. The moonshine was sold by the shot
glass or pint. A bootlegger was a person who sold
moonshine whiskey which was illegal in the state of
Georgia. The bootlegger in our community would hide his
moonshine under everyone's house but his own because
the state men would come to the community searching for
the moonshine under houses and in the bushes or high
weeds. For a long time, I thought the state men were stick
men because they used long sticks with a nail inserted at
the end to look for the moonshine. The moonshine was
placed in tin cans. When the state men were looking for the
moonshine, they used the sticks to push into the high
grass. If the tins were there, the nail would puncture the
can.

"A" is what we called the bootlegger who often tried to
hide the moonshine under our house, but our Chow dog,
Ranger, would bark and run the bootlegger or one of the
men who worked for him away. Someone told my mom
that A had said he was going to poison our dog because he
would not allow the moonshine to be hidden under her

house. He wanted to hide his moonshine under our house and other people's houses because the state men would come to the community looking for the illegal moonshine. If the moonshine was found under someone else's house, they were guilty of the illegal liquor versus A taking the fall.

A was not aware that my mom was raised in the country on a farm. She knew how to shoot a shotgun and a handgun. She always kept a double-barrel shotgun and two handguns in the house. One time, my mother confronted A and told him that he had better hope nothing happened to her dog because she would come looking for him with her double-barrel shotgun. A told everyone that my mother was crazy and not to mess with her because she probably would kill somebody. After mother and A had that "come to Jesus" meeting—compliments to her shotgun—A never attempted to hide moonshine under our house again.

MOONSHINE STORY # 2: POISON MOONSHINE

by Doris Thomas

In the 1950's Black people became ill due to drinking moonshine made by Fat Hardy. Thirty-eight to forty people also died as a result of drinking the liquor.

I can still remember the morning Ann, our next-door neighbor, stumbled onto her front porch, calling my mother for help. We lived next door to Ann in a shotgun house. A shotgun house had a front room, a middle room, and a kitchen. My mother and I were in the middle room when we heard Ann calling my mom. Mother took Ann to the Colored emergency room at Grady Hospital only to find out that she had drunk poisonous whiskey. Ann's brother-in-law was a bootlegger. She and her brother had sneaked into his supply. Late that evening, we found out that people all over the city of Atlanta were sick and dying from poisoned "white lighting." Ann was sent home from the hospital because of a lack of bed space.

I remember hearing Ann's terrifying scream the next morning. We went next door to find her standing on her front porch. She was suddenly blind. The poisoned whiskey had affected her eyesight. Ann died later that evening, leaving a young son. Ann's brother suffered temporary blindness but appeared to recover later. Ladies in the community used gleaners to collect money for Ann's funeral and to purchase clothes for her son to wear to the funeral.

According to an article in the *Atlanta Daily World*, the poisonous moonshine distributed to our next-door neighbor came from John Fat Hardy, a 340-pound white bootlegger who lived in Gainesville, Georgia, north of Atlanta. It was reported by the police that he "cut" the moonshine with methyl alcohol. Fat Hardy received a large order from the Black community in Atlanta and couldn't get it filled by his regular supplier. So, he bought a 55–gallon drum of methyl alcohol which was meant to be used as a fuel additive for racing cars. Fat Hardy juiced it up with a little real moonshine and some fruit flavoring, stirred it up with a broomstick, placed it into barrels, and delivered 77 gallons to the Atlanta Black communities.

The drums he delivered, according to the police, were labeled as both dangerous and poisonous. That's because methyl alcohol is an acutely lethal substance. Methyl alcohol, when drank, metabolizes to formaldehyde and then to formic acid which is poisonous to the central nervous system and may cause blindness, coma, and death. Within hours of consuming Fat Hardy's concoction, Black people were collapsing on the streets and alleyways of Atlanta.

The city's Colored Grady Hospital emergency room was overflowing with sick and dying black patients. Of the 40 who died, 38 were Black residents on Hardy's delivery route, while only 2 were white. Children also consumed the poisonous moonshine but survived. According to reports, some of the first to die were people who lived near the street I lived on. The November 23, 1960 issue of the *Atlanta Daily World* stated that an entire family died from consuming the poisonous moonshine.

Many stories floated around the community where I lived during that time. It was rumored that some black patients who were pronounced dead were pushed aside and later came back to life. It was also said that some patients were still alive when they were injected with formaldehyde.

According to the *Atlanta Daily World,* November 23, 1960, more than 300 people became ill from the poisonous moonshine in an Atlanta area ward that had no liquor stores. Fat Hardy stated he was not aware that methyl alcohol was dangerous despite the warning labels. However, his business partners testified that when people became ill from the first batch of bad whiskey, he retrieved those barrels, poured them into new ones, and sent them out again.

A well-known slogan among moonshiners in north Georgia was, "This liquor was made to sell not to drink." Many shot house operators would not drink the product from their own moonshine stills. It was reported that some "redneck" distillers, who knew their product was destined for the Black community, seemed to get a perverse pleasure in making their liquor as "mean" as possible. This liquor was described as "Nigger Liquor," which they would ship off to Atlanta and to bootleggers of the Black communities and smaller cities.

According to the 2004 spring issue of *Emory Magazine*, an article written by Brent Morgan stated that most bootleggers were white and may have learned their trade from relatives when liquor could not be legally sold in Black communities. Bootleggers would pay off police so they could operate in the Black communities. As a child, I witnessed such a transaction.

Earl Dabney describes the aforementioned event as the most notorious case of illegal alcohol poisoning in American history since the Jake (Jamaica ginger) paralysis days of Prohibition. Fat Hardy's mixture could not be classified as moonshine. It really was a mixture of wood alcohol, but he sold it as the real thing. Fat Hardy, anticipating a heavy drinking weekend throughout Atlanta's Black communities, bought 54 gallons of methyl alcohol at a wholesaler, declaring it was for his service station. From this, Hardy and two friends concocted 77 gallons of alleged white whiskey, which he sold for $4.50 a gallon to three retailers.

It was midnight Sunday when the first victim, after suffering excruciating pain, fell dead of alcohol poisoning. Soon the Colored emergency room and wards of Grady Memorial Hospital were alive with wailing and moaning stretcher cases—terribly sick people whose central nervous systems were deteriorating. They were going blind and all terrified. Thirty-five victims died during the week, and many were left blind and paralyzed.

The editor of the Black Atlanta newspaper, *The Atlanta Daily World*, began notifying the Black community of the poisonous moonshine. He decided to send a delivery truck to Black communities with a megaphone, broadcasting a warning about the liquor. The death toll continued to increase in Atlanta, and the stream of liquor drinkers continued to crowd Grady Memorial Hospital wards. WERD, a local Negro-owned radio station, sounded an hourly alarm against drinking anything but sealed and federally taxed whiskey.

The Atlanta Daily World hired two sound trucks to cruise streets and alleys to warn against drinking moonshine. A 10-year-old male student was rushed from his elementary school to the hospital by a policewoman. He admitted having a drink of corn whiskey at his home and said his parents sold whiskey for a living. He recovered from drinking the poisoned whiskey. A 15-year-old high school girl also drank poisoned liquor. A white man was left blind, and his sister died from the liquor they both drank. His sister had purchased the whiskey from a Negro bootlegger who lived in the rear of her home. One funeral home was reported by the *Philadelphia Tribune* to have had nine bodies laid out in a row as families, friends and curious people viewed them.

On October 24, 1951, a warrant was issued for Fat Hardy's arrest. In an attempt to get out of town, Hardy wrecked his car in rural North Georgia. Hardy was taken to a hospital in Athens, Georgia. He requested to be transferred to Piedmont Hospital in Atlanta, Georgia. He was transferred back to Atlanta to Piedmont Hospital for treatment. The police tracked Hardy down and arrested him in his hospital bed. He was tried and convicted two months later.

Fat Hardy was convicted on December 12, 1951, and sentenced to life in prison by an all-white jury. I remember people in my community saying that Fat Hardy would not receive any time because most of the people murdered were Black. When he was convicted, the Black community said he only received time for the two white people he killed. Fat Hardy escaped from Telfair County Prison camp in 1963 but was recaptured approximately two weeks later. According to the *Atlanta Journal-Constitution*, moonshine consumption went down until Hardy was recaptured. He was released after several failed attempts to obtain parole. Hardy died at the age of 61 after serving 15 years of a life sentence.

I once spoke with a person whose father sold moonshine. She told me that when she was a child, she would go with her father to buy moonshine from a white bootlegger. Blacks had to buy their moonshine on different days than whites. It occurred to me that this gave the moonshiners an opportunity to cut the moonshine with unhealthy additives that could kill or cause illness to Blacks and not whites. The lady I spoke with also told me her uncle and father would pay a white man to buy moonshine for them. They would receive a better quality of moonshine when the white man bought it for them. She said her uncle told her that a man asked her uncle why his moonshine tasted and smelled better than another bootlegger. As a result of witnessing this event as a child, I have no desire to consume any alcohol, even the legal kind.

UNCOVERING THE DRAWING, PART 1

by Doris Thomas

This story shares the process of healing and
overcoming life threatening health issues.

In 1971, I was informed by an orthopedic doctor that I needed to have spinal surgery. I refused to have the surgery because I had just moved into a new house. I was more interested in purchasing furniture and fixing up my home than taking care of my body. As the months passed, it became more difficult to walk and my back pain increased. I was informed that I was running the risk of becoming paralyzed in my right leg. I finally agreed to the surgery with the understanding that I would be returning to work in the next six weeks. However, this did not occur. I remained in the hospital for a month because I developed pneumonia and had to receive blood transfusions. I was unable to walk and had to be turned in my hospital bed by personnel. Once I was released from the hospital, I had a slow recovery.

At home, I was able to do very little for myself. I remember once going outside on the front porch during the day. I was home alone while my children were in school. The street I lived on was empty, and it appeared everyone was at work or inside their homes. After standing outside for a few minutes, I turned to go back inside. But I realized getting back inside the house would be more difficult than coming outside. I could not pick my feet up to get back inside the house. I was at the point of sliding down the wall to the concrete floor, knowing I would not be able to get up until someone came home to help me into the house. Then it occurred to me to lean on the door frame, pull my thigh up, and put my foot inside the door. Finally, I was able to get into the house to return to bed. I was exhausted and slept all afternoon.

When I did not recover as I should have, I was referred to doctors for additional tests and was diagnosed with an illness that progressed faster because of the spinal surgery. I had to learn how to walk again and had to use oxygen. Over the years, I was hospitalized many times but always came through. Due to spinal surgery and other issues, my ability to read dropped to a third-grade level. But I was gradually able to increase my reading level by reading juvenile books, the Bible, and all volumes of *The Lord of the Rings*—a minister gave them to me. He said I probably would not be reading them if I was not confined to the bed and house. I got tired of watching television and soap operas. Because of my illness, I was placed on disability. The doctors said I was too sick to work, and they did not expect me to recover. Before the problem with my back, I was very active. There were many activities to attend in Atlanta that were free for children on Saturdays. After the onset of the pain, our lifestyle changed because I was no longer able to walk and be mobile like I once was. This had a negative impact on my family.

There were three events that led me to attend college. First, I was tired of staying at home all the time. I attended classes for a couple of hours a day, returned home, and got on oxygen and studied. Second, I bargained with God. If He let me live, I would attend college and major in something to help young Black males stay out of jail and prison. I did so by attending college and majoring in criminal justice. Third, President Reagan had just won the election and I feared he would cut people off Social Security, even though they were ill. I felt I needed to obtain an education that would allow me to return to the work force.

In 1980, I took the SAT and began attending Atlanta Junior College, now called Atlanta Metropolitan State College. I started Atlanta Junior College at the same time my fourth child, my son, started Morehouse College.

Atlanta Junior College was a small campus at the time. Many of the students were veterans returning from the Vietnam War. There were single parents mixed in with students just graduating from high school and students taking classes they had failed at the four-year colleges. The professors were very helpful and most had an open-door policy.

I was blessed to only be hospitalized a few times after starting classes and the hospitalizations took place near the weekend. As time went on, I was able to become more involved in campus life at the encouragement of younger students. Because I was a criminal justice major, I was encouraged to join the Criminal Justice Club, and later the Black Psychology Club. I became the manager for the African Dance Club and was one quarter chair of the Writers Club. The advisor for the Black Psychology Club taught Black Psychology, Child Development, and a couple other classes. She was an activist and made us aware of Black History.

Eventually, I was able to work part-time in the Financial Aid office on campus. I made friends with a diverse group of students and learned a lot about other countries. Many students from Africa would bring me gifts when they returned from home. They would give the gifts because I could understand them and was able to assist them. I don't think I will ever forget a pair of blood red thong sandals given to me from Lagos, Nigeria. I literally wore them out.

We formed study groups with single parents and younger students to assist each other with math and other difficult classes. I learned with the study groups that at test time I would remember what we discussed and could easily pass the test. Attending junior college helped to transform me and played a role in my healing process. I was able to graduate with honors and transfer to Georgia State University. I maintained a close relationship with the junior college throughout my time at Georgia State and the University of Georgia. Attending Atlanta Junior College was one of the best decisions I made during that time of my life.

The students and some teachers were very socially conscious about what was going on in our local area as well as the world. Our research and academics centered around what was occurring in the local and larger world and how it impacted us. The students of one white social science professor said she was always telling the young Black females that they would not be able to find a husband to match their educational level. She said that all the Black men were in jail or prison. Allegedly, she had stated that Black females had no Black female role models. She never made those kinds of remarks while I was in her classroom though. I remember asking some of the young women, "Couldn't you have said your mother was your role model?" They said they had not thought of that.

Finally, I was in class one day when the professor made the statement again that Black women would find it difficult to find a husband because all the Black men were in jail or prison. I raised my hand and said I did not expect to have difficulty finding a husband because I would be able to use my degree in criminology to find a husband in prison. Her response was that her statement did not refer to me because she was sure I would find someone. I think Atlanta Junior College added to the foundation I already had and provided information and knowledge I needed to make the transition to begin a new life.

UNCOVERING THE DRAWING, PART 2

by Doris Thomas

*This story shares the process of healing and
overcoming life threatening health issues.*

It seems like a lifetime ago when I took a class at Georgia
State University. The title of the class was Leadership
Through Group. I don't remember the word *group* being a
part of the description of the class in the catalog. For some
reason, I thought this class would allow me to sit in the
back of the classroom, do my work, and not interact with
anyone. I took this class during the summer, so I was a
little tired and just didn't want to be bothered. Much to my
surprise the class was taught through group participation.
We sat in a circle, so everyone could see each other. I was
on a scholarship and needed to take this class.

The first week or two, there were only two Blacks in the
class—a Black male who had a chocolate complexion, large
eyes, and wore his hair in a Jheri curl and me. The class
was asked about their individual goals. When I was asked
this question by the professor, my response was that my
goal was to participate in the class. The professor wanted
to know why that was my goal. My response was that I did
not want to be bothered with a classroom full of Black
students and definitely not a room full of white students.
The professor and students could not believe I had spoken
these words, especially the Black male student. My
statement appeared to make him uncomfortable. One
white female spent the rest of the quarter trying to hold a
conversation with me. I think this was more because of our
similarity in age. Whenever there was a break, she would

make a beeline to me. No matter how hard I tried to avoid her, she still managed to strike up a conversation. I soon accepted that I would be talking with her during breaks.

I did learn something in that class about peeling away layers of baggage that had piled up over several years and seeing what was really there for the first time. I realized it was time to change whatever was underneath the covering.

I started to sew and make clothes prior to enrolling in college and taking the class. I took my children to Six Flags over Georgia where I had a drawing done. I placed the drawing of myself on a wall alongside my sewing machine and began to use it as a bulletin board, using straight pins to tack different things to it—notes, pattern instructions, and other items.

Eventually the drawing was forgotten because of all the things I had pinned atop it. A few years later I decided to remove some of the items I had placed on the drawing. As I removed them, I started to really look at the drawing of myself. I saw something that I had not seen in my face before. First, I saw that the artist had indeed captured my likeness on the drawing paper, but she had somehow also captured the sadness in my eyes and face along with a strange calmness. As I observed the drawing, I wondered why I had not seen this the first time I viewed it. I think I didn't because there was too much going on in my life at that time to recognize it. Just as I covered up the drawing, I covered up things going on in my life.

I believe it is very important that we not cover up or suppress who we are. To do so can lead to many negative issues in our life. Go ahead, be you, and love who you are. Recognize and change the things that work against you or can destroy you. I don't remember why I shared the information about that drawing in the leadership class, but I do remember my professor and classmates making comments that I felt were helpful to me, although I don't remember what they were. The Leadership Through Group class helped me to understand myself and it continues to do so today.

MY MOM AND CIGARETTES

by Doris Thomas

My mom was a heavy smoker when I was a child. This story talks about her overcoming her nicotine addiction.

When I was ten years old, my mom became ill and bedridden from heavy cigarette smoking. My mom smoked a pack a day of Camel cigarettes which led to her having a lung problem. Unfiltered Camels were considered the strongest cigarettes. Dr. A.M. Davis, a Negro doctor, paid my mom house visits for a fee of five dollars per visit. The doctor told my mother she would have to go to Batty State Hospital in Rome, Georgia because her lungs were so bad. He also told her she would need to stop smoking for her lungs to improve. All my life my mom had dealt with headaches. She had sinus surgery at one point but continued to experience headaches. And she took Goody's headache powder almost every day.

Despite the doctor's orders, Mom continued to smoke in bed, so she kept getting weaker. She decided to switch to Kool cigarettes because they were menthol and filtered. I remember going to Danneman's Supermarket on Martin Street to buy cigarettes for her. She smoked one cigarette out of the pack and told me to take them next door to our neighbor. My mother never smoked another cigarette; however, she did put a pinch of Red Bull Tobacco in her cheek to keep nausea down.

When the doctor told my mother that she would have to go to Batty State Hospital for treatment of her lungs, my stepfather asked if he could bring all the supplies needed to her bedside so she could make enough biscuits to last us while she was away. I started asking my mom if I could have different things of hers before she left for the hospital. I didn't really understand how ill my mom was. During the time my mom was ill she asked me to do something. I guess because she was so weak, I thought I could sass her by telling her I was not going to do what she wanted me to do. Well, my mother had a piece of stove wood lying alongside her. She picked up that piece of wood and hit me right between the eyes before I could move. When I came to about a half-hour later, my mom informed me that I was never to sass her.

As a result of my mother stopping smoking, she lived another 35 years. However, we found out that all the smoking weakened the vessels in her brain, causing her to have a brain aneurysm. If she had not stopped smoking, she would have died earlier. About two years before my mom died, I asked her why she stopped smoking. She told me she stopped because she couldn't think of anyone to send us to that who would raise us the way she wanted. She thought her oldest sister had too much going on with her own two children to handle us. Plus, she lived in another state.

My mom thought she had sinus headaches, so she took Goody's headache powder with Coca-a-Cola almost daily. Two of my sons were with her the day she collapsed. Her older grandson, 15 years old, used CPR to start her breathing again. It was assumed that she had died because of a stomach ulcer. I insisted that an autopsy be completed on Mother to find out exactly what she died from. The autopsy revealed that she died from an intracranial aneurysm.

I was glad that I had insisted on the autopsy because I was able to share this information with a cousin who was a heavy smoker. I informed her she needed to stop smoking because of what happened to my mother. She eventually stopped smoking, but not before several intracranial aneurysms had formed and lung disease developed. Fortunately, over the years, a procedure was developed to stop the aneurysms from blowing out. The doctors informed my cousin that the aneurysms were due to her heavy smoking and genetics.

P

by Doris Thomas

*P is the story of a 21-year-old special needs
African American male in the 1950's. P was
loved by the community—adults and
children. P was incarcerated for something
he was not guilty of, and the community
stood with him. He was released, but not
without paying a price.*

In my lifetime, I've come to understand that stories are
very important—especially for families. Stories can dispel
myths and other various misconceptions if they are told in
truth. Stories can be the foundation of staying on track or
getting back on track. For example, my mother had a friend
with a son that some in the community said acted like a
monkey. He was a tall, handsome young man about twenty
years old. Although P was an adult, he acted and played as
if he was about nine or ten years old.

P would run and play with us and ride us on his back.
One day I overheard my mother and P's mother discussing
him. Apparently, P's mother became pregnant while in
high school. She came from an affluent family and was
afraid of what her parents would do to her. To abort the
baby, she drank a mixture of turpentine and Pepsi Cola.
This didn't cause her to miscarry, but, apparently, it was
enough to cause brain damage to the baby. P had the IQ of
a child.

P played with children, but he was also a hard worker.
He worked for Mr. L, a Black man who owned the wood,
coal, and icehouse in the neighborhood. P would cut the

wood into smaller pieces to be used for wood stoves and fireplaces. He also cut 25 and 50 pounds of ice for the ice box and would deliver purchased items to homes in the neighborhood. P cut the wood using a large circular saw that was placed between two stationary pieces of wood. Sometimes children would gather around to watch P cutting the wood.

One day while we were watching P, there were two brothers that were part of the group watching. One of the brothers was considered bad. This brother asked P to cut his finger with the saw. P told him no and to move out of the way. A short time later after this request, P turned his head to pick up another piece of wood while the saw continued to run, and the boy stuck his hand in front of the saw blade cutting up his fingers. P was locked up for cutting the boy's fingers with the saw. On the day of the court hearing, my mom, other community members, and children who were present at the incident attended the hearing. Community people went to court to support P and his parents. P was found not guilty of the incident, but he was castrated because of his low IQ and maybe because he was well endowed. We lived two blocks over from the white housing project. They may have seen him as a threat to the white women in that community. I doubt the judge was concerned for our community.

In the South, Black men were castrated when they appeared to be a threat to white women and men. In some cases, they were castrated then murdered. In recent years, some courts have ordered men who are habitual sexual abusers to undergo injection, hoping that this measure will prevent these men from continuing to sexually abuse others. There was no evidence that P ever had sexual contact with anyone without their consent.

I don't know this for a fact, but when I became older, I think I began to understand why some women in the community would ask P to come by and help them. In fact, I can remember P's mom telling one of them to leave her son alone and that he had the mind of a child. I don't remember much of a change with P after the castration but at my age I probably would not have recognized a change anyway. Many years later after we had moved to another side of town, I saw P downtown with a Bible in his hand preaching on a street corner. I spoke to him and asked how his parents were doing. He gave me that big grin he always had and said they were doing okay.

Our community was very angry with the boy who cut his fingers and his mom. Some of the local children threatened to beat the boy up. Many of the boys in the area had a hard time for a long time. I had not thought about this before, but as I look back, the community attending the court hearing in the 1950's in support of P's family took a lot of courage. Although P was castrated, he was not committed to a mental institution or placed in prison. Some might think the latter two would have been better than the first.

SOUTHEASTERN FAIRGROUND AT LAKEWOOD PARK

by Doris Thomas

*Three children experience fear and terror
walking home one night from the fairground.*

I was born in the old Colored Grady Hospital in Atlanta, Georgia which is not the Grady Hospital currently standing today. The Colored Grady Hospital was a red building located on the corner of Butler Street and Armstrong Street. The house I lived in from birth was six miles from the hospital. I remember the places I lived with fond memories, but the area I lived in from third to ninth grade had a profound impact on my life. Many call these years the "formative years." They had a great deal to do with who I am today. I recently shared this story at a family gathering with my brother present. I didn't think he remembered the event, but he did and concurred with my rendition of it.

When I was growing up, there was a fair held every fall at the Southeastern Fairground at Lakewood Park in Atlanta. This was during segregation. Negroes were only allowed to attend the fair on two days. The rest of the days were for whites only. We went to the fair on the last day for Negroes. Students were given a coupon to attend but it had to be used by a certain time before the entrance price increased. My friend, Hattie, and I were in the eighth grade at the time. Our mothers decided the two of us were old enough to attend the fair alone with my brother. Once we arrived home from school, my brother, Hattie, and I walked about two blocks to catch the trolley.

Once at the fair, we discovered the cost to enter had increased and we did not have enough money for all of us to attend. Even if we all got in, we still would not have enough to get something to eat, ride a ride, and play a game or two. I made a sacrifice and decided not to go in. I divided my money up between Hattie and my brother but kept a dime for the trolley ride home. I reminded them both to save money for trolley fare and to leave before dark and I would wait outside the gate. Unfortunately, they did neither.

When they came out, I asked them why they had not come out when it started to get dark. They claimed they were having such a good time and forgot. They also told me they had spent their trolley money. I got angry and told them I was going to leave them and catch the trolley home. Both began to cry because neither knew the way home from the fairgrounds. To tell the truth, I wasn't sure if I knew the way home either.

We started the long walk and soon realized we had walked in a circle. A white truck with several young white boys standing in the bed were banging on the roof top and yelling loudly as they passed us. They looked as if they were drinking alcohol. I told my brother and Hattie we had to hide because they may come back for us. We hid in a deep ditch. The truck did return, driving slowly. I could see the boys were looking around for us. I don't know how long we stayed in that ditch, but we eventually came out and resumed walking.

By then I had a better idea of the direction home, but I still wasn't completely sure. The Lakewood Fairgrounds were in Lakewood Heights, and we lived in Summerhill about two blocks from the state capitol. After we walked for about eight or nine blocks, a young Negro man driving a black car stopped and asked if we wanted a ride. I told him no because we didn't know him. Hattie and my brother thought we should have accepted the ride and became angry with me for not taking it. We continued to walk. When we were about halfway home, we saw the young man leaning on his car in front of a juke joint talking to Stumpy Joe and three other men. Joe was called Stumpy Joe because his right leg was amputated, and he had a peg leg. We were hurt and upset that we did not accept the ride.

The young man just smiled at us and Stumpy waved. We finally reached our home, and our parents were very angry. Once we explained what had happened, they calmed down. The three of us ended up with blisters on our feet.

After I told this story, family members and friends asked me why I gave my brother and Hattie my money. My response was that there was not enough money for all of us to ride the rides and get something to eat. I didn't really have a problem with sitting outside and waiting for them. Someone asked why I didn't hold their trolley fare. I could not recall if it was because I didn't think of it at the time or because we didn't have the correct change to divide. When I started to write the account of this event, I decided to research the Southeastern Fair and found pictures of it and the area where we started walking. I can only say the grace of God was surely with us that night.

THE NEW BABY

by Doris Thomas

When I was in elementary school, my mother was informed that her sister had given her newborn baby girl to a nurse at the hospital. My mother said, "No child in our family was going to be given to a stranger." My mom went to the hospital and brought the three-day old baby home. I fell in love with the baby instantly and was happy to help take care of her. My mom was not working when she first came to live with us. When she did return to work, I was responsible for taking my cousin to daycare before I went to school and picking her up after school.

During the summer, my baby cousin became ill when she was between 10 months and one year of age. She was still young enough to be placed in a crib. The crib we had was the metal type. Back then, the old Colored Grady Hospital only had wards, so cribs were all alongside the walls. The doctors said she had pneumonia and was placed in a "croup tent" to help her breathe and stop coughing. For some reason, it was decided that I was the reason she had developed pneumonia. My cousin would not let the nurses or aides feed her, so I had to go to the hospital to feed her breakfast and lunch. My mother usually fed her in the evening after she got off work.

We lived about two or three blocks from the state capitol. At that time there was a housing project for whites called Capitol Homes. The apartments sat on three corners with a soda fountain on the fourth corner. The soda fountain was for whites only. Every day on my way to the hospital there would be a group of white children of various ages sitting on the front porch of the apartments.

One day, on my way to feed my cousin her lunch, a white boy on the porch called me a nigger. I was already angry because I had to walk to the hospital and without thinking I ran up on the porch after the boy. He ran into the apartment, but I ran after him, hit him, and then ran out. I think the others were so shocked they didn't react to what had happened.

After that incident I didn't walk in that direction again because I was afraid that they would beat me up. After a few days I told some of the boys in the neighborhood what had happened. They decided I should walk ahead of them, so they would not be seen. When I reached the apartments, the children came out ready to beat me up. The boys from my neighborhood came running out and we all fought until we heard the police siren. All of us ran in different directions—negroes and whites. I had to walk out of the way for the rest of my cousin's stay in the hospital.

BABY II

by Doris Thomas

My cousin lived with us until she was six years old when her mom returned to take her back. At first, my mom told my cousin, *no,* but my aunt called the police and told them my mom had taken insurance out on her daughter and intended to kill her. My mother had taken educational, life, and accidental life insurance policies out on my brother, my cousin, and me when we were first born. The only thing that kept my mother out of jail was the insurance man, an agent of a Black owned insurance company. He had known my mother since we were born and informed the investigator that if my mom was going to hurt any of us, she would have done it a long time ago. My aunt was allowed to take my cousin but was not allowed to keep the insurance—neither was my mom.

THE BREAK IN

by Doris Thomas

I arrived home from the doctor feeling depressed, tired, upset, and angry about the diagnosis I received. I owned a car but was told by the doctor that I should not drive. I continued to drive until I was informed by the doctor that if I was not concerned about having an accident and injuring myself, I should be concerned that I could be responsible for injuring or killing someone else if I lost consciousness while driving. I was receiving oxygen at the time. The doctor's latter statement convinced me I should stop driving. Due to my inability to drive, I had to take the bus to my doctor's appointment. By car, the trip was 25 to 30 minutes, but the bus trip was two hours. Afterwards I was tired and decided to take a nap, hoping to feel better when I woke up. I had not been in bed for more than a few minutes when I heard a noise at the back door. I thought to myself, *I am not going to the door—they will go away.* About a minute later I could hear the doorknob being shaken. I got out of bed and went into the kitchen to see who was at the back door. The back door was wood at the bottom, but the top was glass with a screen on the outside. As I entered the kitchen, I saw a man standing at the backdoor and a man at the dining room window which was low to the ground. Both were trying to get into the house.

When I walked into the kitchen, both stopped trying to enter my house. The man at the back door asked for a man whose name I was not familiar. I informed him that no one lived here by that name. But instead of them leaving, the man at the backdoor really attempted to get the door open. By this time, I was very angry and frustrated. I was ready to kill both men. *How dare they violate my home in this way?*

I must have looked out of it for them to think they could continue to enter my home with me standing there talking to them. It was a warm day, and school was in session, so there was no activity on the street. My mom and aunt were raised on a farm, and they believed in having a weapon in the home. My aunt died and left her shotgun to my mom. My mom died a year later, leaving me my aunt's double barrel shotgun. My mom left me her 22-caliber pistol and a silver automatic. I stumbled back to the bedroom and searched the closet for the shotgun. I loaded that shotgun with shells and started to close the butt of it, but it would not close. I decided to hold the shotgun in a way that the intruders could not see that the butt was not close.

When I returned to the kitchen and turned the corner, the man at the door saw the barrels of the shotgun, and he yelled to the man that I had a shotgun. Both he and the man at the window ran to a car parked on the side of the house. After they drove away, the butt of the shotgun snapped into place. Afterwards I was very thankful I was unable to close the shotgun. Although I was angry with the men who were trying to break in, I am glad I didn't have to deal with possibly killing one or both. I am forever grateful to God I was unable to fire that shotgun.

I have often wondered if people think about the state of mind a person might be in when they are contemplating a crime against them. That possible victim may be going through something that is causing them to be angry or depressed. This could cause them to react violently against the person committing the crime against them rather than being afraid of them. If I had not had guns, I would have done an "Al Green" and thrown some boiling water or some type of chemical in the kitchen on the man at the door. Never underestimate the power of a crazed woman.

Later, I learned that the men were arrested for a string of burglaries in the community. I was also informed that the burglaries were taking place because the community was going through a transition due to "white flight." Whites were moving out of the neighborhood at a rapid rate because African Americans were moving in. People in the community were not familiar with their neighbors. Once neighbors became familiar with one another, the community stabilized and the burglaries stopped. I am sure the arrest of those two men contributed to a reduction in crime also.

BELL EMPLOYMENT AGENCY

by Doris Thomas

In the late 1950s, when I was about sixteen or seventeen years old, I went to the Bell Employment Agency to look for a job. The agency hired colored people to fill various positions. I was hired as a babysitter to take care of one-week-old twins and a three-year-old girl while the mother went out. I was shocked because, at that time, colored mothers did not leave their one-week-old babies to go shopping. Babies needed to be at least four to six weeks old for a mother to leave the home. It was believed it was unsafe for women and their babies to be exposed to the public. I was also surprised to find her husband at home. I wondered why they needed a babysitter if he was going to be home. In addition to babysitting, I was to wash dishes and clean the kitchen.

The husband kept his distance until his wife left home. The three-year-old came into the kitchen while I washed the dishes. Once his wife left the house, the husband came into the kitchen and started to talk to me. I was not used to talking to strange men, colored or white. This made me very uncomfortable. It was awkward holding a conversation with that man.

At some point, he came up close behind me, and I looked back to see his penis exposed. I was so upset and frightened, I left immediately without receiving payment for the work I had done. I was not sure where I was because the wife had picked me up from the bus stop and was supposed to take me back to it at the end of the day. I had not really paid attention to the surroundings as we drove straight to their subdivision. After walking for a little while, I was able to find my way out of the subdivision and to the bus stop. I did not tell my mom because I did not want her to get into trouble.

The next day, I went back to the Bell Employment Agency. I informed the colored receptionist of the prior day's event. The receptionist stated she had wondered why ladies did not return to the household, nor did they contact the agency afterward. The family had requested Bell Employment Agency to send three different young women to work for the couple before sending me. Thankfully, the receptionist paid me for the work performed the day before for the couple.

My next employment opportunity was gained through answering a want ad in the *Atlanta Journal-Constitution* newspaper. The ad stated they were seeking a young, colored girl to work in a photography studio. In those days, an ad might also state "only light skin" but this one read "colored should apply." When I interviewed for the job, I was informed that I would be taught how to develop film and other duties related to photography. The owner was an older white man—at least he looked old to me—with a large round girth. If I remember correctly, his hair was gray. This was around 1960. He brushed up against me while teaching me how to develop film in the dark room. I thought his touching me could have been accidental because of the tight space. However, he finally made a sexual advance towards me. I informed him I was not interested and left.

It was not until recently that I realized the want ads and employment agencies were probably used by many people who were predators to lure black female minimum wage earners. Some suffered sexual assault while others may have been raped or even murdered and went missing without their families being aware of what happened to them.

LOVE AT ANY AGE

by Doris Thomas

Nzinka walked out of the doctor's office into the noon day sun. Hoping that the sun would rejuvenate her, she thought of how she had jokingly said she must have been a sun goddess in her past life, because of the ways the sun always seemed to give her strength. If ever she needed strength, she needed it now.

There was a small park across the street where she found a bench directly in the sun. She sat down, wondering what to do about her situation. It was bad enough to be pregnant at her age, but under the circumstances, she felt it was just too much. Many thoughts ran through her mind. Should she think of her pregnancy as a problem and treat it as one? Or should she tell the father so they can decide together on what they want to do?

Nzinka had always relied on her own strength, but this time she wondered if she needed his strength. As she turned these questions over in her mind, she thought of the first time they had gone out together. They had known each other for three months when he took her out to celebrate their birthdays. By the time they had their first date, they were close friends. In fact, the first time she met him, he made an impression on her. She thought that he was very nice. However, someone else came into Nzinka's life and she dismissed him from her thoughts. Months later, after that affair was over, she ran into him again and decided to go to dinner with him later in the week. But because of their busy schedules, it took almost a month before they could get together.

To celebrate their birthdays, they went to a small restaurant with candlelit tables. Since her birthday had just passed, age came into the conversation. He still teased her about her reaction and the expression on her face when he told her his age. She almost choked on the wine that she was sipping, and she could feel her eyes widening. His reaction to all this had been that he was a mature adult male and felt that age was just a number. Yet she thought the age gap between 27 and 40 was fairly wide—she being the one who was 40. She thought to herself, my God, how did I get into this and vowed to never see him again. She told him she couldn't possibly date anyone as young as him—not at her age. But then she found herself going out with him and enjoying being with him more and more. When he was depressed about problems, she found she wasn't happy until she had brought him out of his saddened state.

When he told her that he had become too close to her, she told him she understood and said goodbye to him. Since that conversation had taken place on the phone, it was easy to do so. As the years passed, she regretted telling him goodbye, but she decided she would stick to it.

One week he called and asked if she was angry. She said no, and the affair instantly resumed. She knew and understood what was taking place with him. They both had started to care more than they wanted. Neither wanted to give as much as they were giving in terms of emotions. Both were trying to fight the way they felt about each other. She thought of the poem he had inspired her to write. How he had smiled and wanted to frame the rough draft copy because he had been the inspiration for it.

All these things flooded through her mind as she wondered to herself, *how can such a thing happen to me?* She was just beginning to enjoy herself, like never before. *How could she allow a baby into her life? And what about him?* Although he had asked her to marry him, she still didn't feel secure enough with herself to accept the age difference in a marriage. With a baby, would she have the energy to spend time with him? She did feel in the best of health, but her mind was in turmoil as all these thoughts flooded through it. What would she do?

After sitting for what seemed an eternity, she stood up and looked toward the sun. Her strength was renewed, and she headed for home.

MY FAVORITE MALE COUSIN

by Doris Thomas

Ely and my mother were the children of two sisters, making them first cousins. Ely was one of two male relatives that I knew growing up. The other male relative was an uncle by marriage—he married my mother's oldest sister. They lived in the state where my mother was born. Ely was about six feet six inches tall with wide shoulders and wavy, crinkly shoulder-length hair when it was not straightened out with a straightening comb. His complexion was that of a reddish color with a touch of bronze. I adored Ely. He was my hero. Ely grew up with my mom in Alabama, and I remember him living in Atlanta, but then he disappeared for a while. My mom said he had gotten into trouble and had gone home to Alabama to hide out.

As I grew older, there were events in my cousin Ely's life that concerned me. Although I loved him, it became difficult for me to like him. I was very young, about five years old, the first time I heard a story about my cousin. We were living upstairs over a tavern. Apparently, he had beaten his common-law wife, Bill, and pushed her down some stairs in front of a moving truck. Fortunately, the truck driver saw Bill and swerved before he hit her. The driver said he saw my cousin Ely push Bill, but she testified that she stumbled and fell into the path of the oncoming truck.

Bill continued to live with Ely, even under such abusive circumstances. I don't remember seeing Ely again until we moved to Summerhill where he was still living with Bill. Cousin Ely would beat Bill for no good reason at all. One time, it was because he didn't think she had straightened his hair right. Those events took place in the 1950s. My mom gave Bill some money so she could leave Ely, but she refused to leave him. When Ely found out about my mom giving Bill money, he never said anything or questioned my mom, but he took it out on Bill and beat her again.

I'll never forget one particular incident between Ely and Bill. Ely was a carpenter by trade, so he had a big bag of tools. One of his tools was a leveler; it was large and long with metal on all sides. Ely became angry with Bill for some reason, and he used the leveler to beat her. I remember going with my mom to see her in the ward of the old Colored Grady Hospital. Bill's leg was in traction, her arm was in a cast, and she had a bandage around her head. She also had a black eye. I liked Bill so it really hurt me to see her in that condition. That beating left Bill crippled with one leg shorter than the other. Once again, my mom tried to get Bill to press charges against our cousin, but she refused.

Ely and Bill lived behind us at the top of a hill. The area had a wall made of stones. People were able to jump from the wall to the lower level. After Bill was discharged from the hospital, my mom would take Bill food and check in on her. This happened during the summer months and one day I heard someone knocking on our screen door. I went to the door and saw two white men standing there. They wanted to know if I knew where to find Ely. I had just looked out the back door and had seen Ely standing on the stone wall.

Although I was a child, I was going to show them where Ely was standing because of what he had done to Bill. But before I could tell them where Ely was one of the men said, "I understand that nigger loves his long hair. We can't wait to cut it all off." The man spoke with so much vindictiveness, I immediately decided not to help them nor tell them where my cousin was located. That was the last time I saw my cousin. However, my mother stayed in contact with Bill for a short time afterwards.

Bill moved in with a man who was an above the knee double amputee. The only difference in this man and my cousin Ely, was that he was in a wheelchair. He still treated Bill in the same manner that Ely had. He would wait until Bill was close enough to him to grab her by her dress or pant leg. He would then pull her to him and beat her. By this time, I was a preteen and began to wonder what was wrong with Bill that she would allow someone to subject her to that type of treatment. We moved from the area and didn't see her for a long time.

Years later my mother ran into Bill, and she informed my mother that she was no longer with the man in the wheelchair. In fact, she had decided to not allow any man to abuse her physically or verbally anymore.

As a young girl, after the abuse that I had witnessed between my cousin and his common–law wife, I thankfully was not exposed to this kind of domestic violence until much later in life. Seeing this type of violence and abuse made me angry and aware of this type of behavior, so I was determined not to allow it to happen to me.

According to mom, my cousin beat Bill on a regular basis, but I remember my mom telling another story about Ely and how he beat another woman. Ely had left after beating this woman and then returned to make up with this woman. While she was hugging him, she used a razor that she had concealed behind her back in her other hand. Apparently, she was trying to decapitate him. The woman slit his throat from his ear halfway around his neck. The incident happened so quickly, and the woman left before Ely realized she had cut him. For those of you who don't know this, you don't feel the cut of a razor blade when the cut is occurring. Ely survived, but because he was so fair skinned, the razor cut only left a thin scar circling halfway around his neck.

Thankfully, I never lived in an abusive family, nor saw my mom get hit or be abused by a man. This story instilled in me that loving me is one thing but hitting me does not equal caring for me. I decided I would never allow anyone to take advantage of me in that way.

SCHOOL DAYS

by Jacqui Jones

I made my debut on a very hot day in July—July 25th to be precise. Mama told me later, when I was five years old, that it was 100 degrees that day. I guess that's why I love summer and really can't stand the cold winter months.

I was the first born of four—two boys and two girls. We all came in two-year increments except for my baby sister who decided she would change the schedule and add a year before she appeared on the scene. That meant I was two when my oldest brother was born, four when baby brother came along, and seven with baby sis. Now being the first born should come with some nice perks and privileges, like being the most loved one or the favorite child. Not so in my case—baby sis got all the perks. I was bestowed with the honor of having ALL the responsibility.

When I was eight, Mama decided to go to back school to become a nurse. I'll never forget that day. Mama sat me down and said, "Jacqueline"—she always called me by my given name when she wanted my full attention— "I'm going to need your help. I'll be depending on you." I'm thinking, *I'm eight, what can I do?* Well, I soon found out. First, Mama taught me how to cook simple meals like breakfast—oatmeal or cold cereal with bacon and toast. Lunch was usually just sandwiches and milk. By the time I was 10 years old, I could fix dinner if needed. I also became the babysitter and "substitute Mom" for my siblings. There were no child protection laws back in the 1950s, so we were left home alone while Mama went to school and Daddy worked. Of course, if something came up that I couldn't handle, I had instructions to go next door and get Miss Jackson.

Somehow, we kids survived, so I guess I did a good job. But I must say, I always hated being the oldest. I secretly wished that I had a big brother to watch over and take care of me, especially when I had to deal with the neighborhood bully when I was nine years old. This girl was three years older and very big for her age. She seemed to get great pleasure out of punching me in my stomach for no reason every day on my way home from school. My oldest brother, the tattletale, told Mama that I was coming home crying all the time.

I don't know why I didn't tell her. Probably because I remembered her saying she depended on me so that meant I couldn't be a cry baby. Anyway, Mama got so mad.

"Why are you letting some girl hit you?" she yelled.

My response, "I don't know."

Mama said, "Well, young lady, I don't want to hear about anymore crying from you. If I do, it's me you will have to deal with."

Now, I'll tell you I was more afraid of Mama than I was of the bully. I put some deep thought into what to do about Miss Bully. Like clockwork the next day, I saw Miss Bully coming down the street toward me, but I could hear Mama's words repeating in my mind, *no crying or you'll have to deal with me.* Before Miss Bully could get her punch in, I picked up a brick that just happened to be lying in front of me and threw it at her. *BAM!* That brick hit her right upside the head. She was on the ground with blood running down the side of her face. I took off running toward my house. My brother was surprised to see me not crying. Not a tear dropped from my eyes. In fact, I left the scene with a big smile on my face.

Needless to say, I never had any more problems with Miss Bully. I didn't realize at the time but that was a life lesson learned. The lesson was to always confront your problems head on—with a brick if necessary.

THE KISS

by Jacqui Jones

Well, here I am, ten years old and in my fifth-grade classroom. It's around 10:00 am and Ms. Packard, my teacher, is at the front chalkboard, writing something that I guess I should be paying attention to. But my mind is on Robert, a student who sits two rows over toward the front—I have a good view of him. Now, Robert, of course, doesn't even know that I exist. I don't think he's into girls. I once heard him tell his friend that girls were nothing but pains in the butt. However, I think he just said that because he's never experienced what a girl can do up close and personal.

I hear Ms. Packard say, "Class, open your books to page ..." but I don't hear the rest. My focus is back on Robert, the tallest boy in the class. He is very cute. *As I think back on this, I have always liked and still do, my men to be tall. Anyway, back to Robert.* I'm thinking, I sure would like for him to be my boyfriend, but how do I do it? Recess is coming up at 10:30, and I am a tomboy. Maybe I could get close to him by playing ball with the boys instead of jumping double Dutch with the girls. That's it!!! The perfect plan!

Now I'm watching the clock—come on 10:30. I have no idea what Ms. Packard has been talking about all morning. Yes, finally there's the recess bell. We're all running for the door. The boys are on one side of the playground and the girls on the other. I go over to the boys' side close to Robert.

"What do you want?" he asks. "Go back with the girls."

I defend myself, "I'm a good player. Pick me for your team."

He looks at me with a frown like he's seeing me for the first time.

"Okay, go over there," he says, pointing to his team.

Yes, my plan is working!

We play ball for about 10 minutes then recess ends. As we're walking back to class, Robert whispers that he'll walk me home after school today.

The rest of the day was a total blur. I'm really only concerned with the day being over and walking home with Robert.

Yay, there's the bell!

Ms. Packard says, "Class dismissed!"

Robert is standing outside waiting for me. This is so great! We walk home—I'm only about two blocks away from school. I don't think we said a word along the way. When we got to my house, I thanked Robert for walking me home. He leaned in close and kissed me on the lips, then ran away. What?! Robert does like me. This has no doubt officially been the best day of my life.

RACISM

by Jacqui Jones

My mother and father had been saving as much as they could for 10 years. That's not easy to do when you have four children and two of them went to Catholic school which meant extra money going to tuition. Add to this the fact that Dad LOVED to play the horses. I can remember some very heated arguments when Mama let him have it for gambling away ALL the rent money.

Today is a special day. Dad came home with McDonald's meals for all of us. That hardly ever happens. Dad said he had a big announcement. Mama was still at work. She's now a nurse and works the 3:00 p.m. to 11:00 p.m. night shifts. I'm eleven years old and can't really remember Dad spending any time with us kids. It seemed like he was always working. He worked the swing shift at Chicago's steel mill and didn't think twice about pulling a double shift when it was offered. So, I'm wondering what's up. Dad said that he and Mama just bought a new house. *Wow! That is exciting news.* Up to now, we have always lived in apartments. Currently, we live in a four-story, large courtyard building in a three-bedroom apartment on the 4th floor.

It was a quick move. Two weeks later, we are in the new house, but there are a few details Dad forgot to mention. First, the house isn't anything like I had imagined. I had pictured a ranch house like the ones I always see on TV, for instance on the show *Leave it to Beaver*. This is a two-story bungalow. Second, we moved into an all-white neighborhood. We are the only Blacks on the block. Our tenants on the second floor are white but they soon leave when they find out their new landlord is Black.

Being in an all-white neighborhood means we have to attend a white school. Until now, I have never really been exposed to white people, so I'm totally unprepared for how they'll act towards me. It's the late 1950s and most white people do not like Black people at all.

Before long, I experienced some very traumatic and scary things. I'm only eleven and in the sixth grade. It's just me and one other Black girl, Nana, in class. It's the first day, and all the white kids are calling us nigger—dirty nigger, nasty nigger, and black nigger. They refuse to sit by us in the lunchroom or play with us at recess time. Not only are the white kids horrible but the white teachers also have attitude and make it very clear that they don't like the idea of having Black kids in their class. Nana and I are in Hell every day.

I can't wait to get away from school on this first day. I went home to tell my parents about what happened. I can tell that Dad is really hurt. Dad grew up in the deep, deep South in Mississippi and remembered all that stuff with the Ku Klux Klan. He ran away from home to the North when he was just seventeen. However, I get no sympathy from Mama. She tells me that I just have to stick it out because we are not going to move anywhere. My sixth-grade year was the worst. Having to endure all this prejudice at eleven years old makes me an evil, mean child. I learn quickly to HATE white people.

Fortunately, the neighborhood changes over time. "White Flight" is what real estate people call it. Blacks keep moving in and the whites run out just as fast. I'm in seventh grade now, and there are some big, strong Black boys enrolled in school. They aren't taking any mess from the white kids and began issuing out butt whippings as necessary. I am so glad to see these strong Black boys handling business. They even know how to handle the most racist, prejudice teacher in the whole school—Ms. Cole, the teacher who accidentally touched me one day as she was passing out some papers. She immediately ran to the washroom to wash her hands. Guess she thought she was going to turn Black or something from touching me. However, my Black boys fixed her. One day after school, she discovered her car wouldn't start. Seems someone had poured a whole five-pound bag of white sugar down her gas tank. That was the best laugh I've had in years. She never did find out who did it. But all the Black kids knew, and we were not telling.

Mom and Dad

Thanks to my new Black classmates, I made it through seventh and eighth grade to graduate. But now the school board has decided they are not going to deal with this racial problem at the high school level. They simply change and redraw the boundary lines for attendance to their "lily white" high school to make sure no Blacks could attend. Now I go to an all-black high school which is perfectly fine with me.

HIGH SCHOOL

by Jacqui Jones

Wow, I'm in my first year of high school. "Freshies" are what freshmen are called by the senior class. The seniors consider themselves much too important to speak to or associate with mere freshies. There are also other groups that freshies are excluded from like the sports teams—basketball, football, wrestling, and even the cheerleading squad. Then you have the scholastic clubs like the chess club that is composed of super smart kids and the language clubs–Spanish, French and German. So, we freshies decided to form our own club and band together for activities.

Freshies eat lunch together and attend the basketball and football games as a group. There are about fifty of us out of the original 300 freshies that hang out together, so we're okay. Fortunately for me, since I attended an all-white grammar school for two years from the sixth through eighth grade, I am now very advanced scholastically—the only advantage of attending a white school. I tested as functioning at the junior high school level when I started because I had higher level skills. I was allowed to join the Spanish club. It felt good to be part of a special group, but I prefer to hang out with my freshie friends.

One of the fun things in high school is the "sock hops." These are the dances that the school staff sponsors four times a year. The sock hops are held in the gym and are always chaperoned. They usually happen on a Friday at the end of a school day between 1:00 p.m. and 3:00 p.m. At the dance, we take off our shoes and dance in our socks, thus the name sock hop. Most of the time, we have some of the top Chicago DJs spinning records.

I love sock hops because they are my opportunity to get close to the boys. Sure, I'm a tomboy but that doesn't mean I'm not interested in boys for other purposes. I'm noticing boys much more now—especially which boys are cute and which ones are not.

Of course—as a teenager—everything is based on physical appearance. In the 1960s, especially in the Black community, if you are light-skinned, it is a major advantage. Even though I was not of light skin, it seems I was drawn to the light-skinned boys. As I think back on it, all those special school clubs I mentioned earlier had members that were of lighter skin, and this was especially true of the cheerleaders.

At the sock hop, I dance with all the boys that are "free," meaning unattached. All the sports team boys are always with their girlfriends, so they are off limits. We had so much fun doing all the popular dances from the 1960s—the Twist, the Monkey, the Bop, and the Bus Stop, which was the very first line dance.

Freshman year was all good and nothing but big fun. Too bad I can't turn time back and relive it one more time taking everything I know now back with me. Sophomore and junior years are mostly uneventful. They are not about having fun but rather getting down to business and deciding what courses and curriculum I need to be studying. I'm planning to go to college so that means taking the necessary classes for admittance—two years of a language, three years of some type of math, for example algebra, geometry, and calculus, as well as chemistry, biology, and four years of English. I was an "A" student, so I had no problem passing these subjects.

It's now my senior year, and I have all the requirements out of the way so I can enjoy the fun that occurs during senior year.

The main event occurring toward the end of senior year is the senior prom. Prom will be the first time I attend a formal dinner dance. I'm having so much fun shopping for my full-length gown and all the accessories. *This was also the year that I met the boy that would eventually become my husband. It's funny how meeting a particular person can cause drastic changes in your life's plans. It's because of this one boy that I didn't go to college until much later in life.* Prom and graduation are over, and I get married right after high school,  and I do mean right after—literally a month after I turned eighteen. *I think about that now—I graduated at 17, got married at 18, and then I was pregnant within three months. What was I thinking?*

My baby is two years old now, and I'm still a stay-at-home mom. It's time I made some major changes in my life. I got a job working nine to five in the corporate world and attend school at night to earn my college degree. Of course, going to school on a part-time basis means it takes me much longer to obtain my degree, but after six years of struggling, I am a college graduate. I finally made it. I am so proud of myself for attaining my Bachelor's in Business Administration.

A MOTHER'S INFLUENCE

by Helen Benton Brown

Ecclesiastes states there is a time, a season, and a purpose for everything under the heavens, and God does all things well. My life reflects this notion, specifically with my mothers, as they were there for me for a time, a season, and a purpose.

My natural mother, Dorothy Ellen Powe Benton, gave birth to sixteen children, and I was number eleven. She was a very wise and caring woman who had a unique relationship with each of her children, loving them equally—no one more than the other. She fought for justice and education. She taught us that we could achieve and become all that we desired if we put our minds to it. When we failed at things we attempted, she always hugged us, told us she was proud of us, and encouraged us to do it again or try something different.

She rose early to meditate, pray, and prepare breakfast. She barely worked outside of the home and was always there when we left for school and when we returned. Her smile is still fresh in my mind. I stayed very close to her during my pre-teen and teenage years because she had a lot to share about life. Her conversations were more

151

important than those I had with my friends at the time. As her health began to deteriorate due to allergies and bronchial asthma in my last two years of high school, I often accompanied her to the emergency room during the midnight hours. She never let others see the pain of her condition—her smile took it all away.

When I was in the sixth grade, I remember telling Mother that I was going to college.

She looked at me and said, "Your two oldest sisters said the same thing and instead they moved to New York and got married. So, wait until you are in the twelfth grade and let me know what you are going to do."

That is exactly what I did. I announced to her before I graduated that I would be going to college in the fall. After applying to three colleges of my choice, I chose Elizabeth City State University in Elizabeth City, NC. The moment arrived that August morning for me to leave and Mother announced to me that she would not be going. Instead, my brother, Robert, would be taking me. She hugged me and told me I would do well.

That was the scariest moment of my life and the last time I saw her alive. I refused to cry, but my heart was heavy. Mom passed away seven days after I left for college. I'd lost my best friend. Looking back, I will always remember her for the many things she did for us—the tears she shed to save us, her heart of pure gold, her eyes of love light shining, and how right she was in all that she shared. She did not live to be old but to be wiser. Mother was there in my life at the right time, for a season, and for a good purpose. I honor her for my early years of development. I am who I am today because of her guidance, nurturing, and perfect love.

As my life continued its course, I moved to Brooklyn, NY where I encountered Mother Lillian Brown. She was another beautiful woman of God. She had six children of her own, yet she took me in anyway and began to train me in church life. She taught me how to take a little and make a lot—to be creative with the gifts I had. She taught me how to accomplish a lot in a short period of time and to always be ready for the Lord's work.

Mother Brown gave the best hugs. She could scold you and laugh at the same time. As an adult, whenever I visited, I never wanted to leave. Her input was invaluable. I will always remember her for the laugh that I still hear today, for the instructions she carefully taught, her heart of pure love, the light that gleamed from her eyes, the impartation from the word of God, the answers that always made sense, and the nod she would give as her approval. Mother Brown was there at the right time in my life, for a season, and for a purpose. I honor and thank her for showing me life from a different perspective.

Another wonderful mother was Patsy Reily, the one who helped enhance my administrative abilities. She will always be a great friend. She never gave a harsh word. She listens intently and corrects with love. One of the greatest gifts she gave me is preparing me for life. The closeness we share is untouchable.

Patsy has four sons. I will always remember her for the patience she exhibited while training me, along with her ability to be in charge and delegate responsibilities. Her teachings on being a mother, grandmother, wife, sister, and friend were invaluable. She taught me how supporting your husband in his career gets you what you want. Finally, she made me understand that no matter how many years of experience one has, it means nothing unless you are healthy. She was there for a time and purpose. I honor her for continuing to nurture and guide me towards my destiny.

Mothers, mothers everywhere.

"Will you wear my wedding dress from 51 years ago?" asked, Doreen Clark, an extraordinary woman who became a lifelong friend.

"Yes, I will," I replied, joyfully.

I met Doreen through my brother, Jerome, who introduced me to her. She has four children and is the feistiest person I have ever met, and I mean that in a good way. She speaks her mind and will not back down. Like her son, Jerome, she loves to hug, and so do I. Her knowledge of nature, plant life, and outdoor living has given me a glimpse into the secrets of longevity.

Life is full of changes, yet changes are necessary for us to grow. I will forever cherish Doreen for taking dominion in the Kingdom of God, for the Divine Order she keeps in the trunk of her car, the rapport she has with people, her eyes of love that are ever searching for me, her ears that hear the smallest words, and her palm nestled in mine every Sunday at mass give me a genuine feeling of being loved. Doreen is here for a time and purpose. I honor her for filling in the gaps in my life.

I am eternally grateful for the mothers that were a positive force in my life as they helped me to become an individual who is healthy, excited, loving, and encouraging to others. These women are celebrated as are others who help shape, mold, teach, train, nurture, and guide all of us into the wonderful human beings we have and will become. They are the backbones of life and the strength of our nation. Well done, mothers! Thank you for your love and influence.

NOW I KNOW WHY

by Beatress C. Lynn

This is the story of losing one's innocence at a tender age, facing shame and guilt while finding the strength to persevere through the love of God and the power of forgiveness.

I want to tell my story. Maybe I can help someone else free themselves so they can understand that what happened to them is not their fault. I realize that there are lots of children who are now grown men and women who blame themselves for the abuse they experienced. Finally, at 64 years old, I have gotten to the point where I can talk about what happened to me—I was molested by my own father at a very young age.

When I was seven years old—I didn't think anything about it at the time—but my dad would tickle me and make me laugh until I cried. It did not hurt. It actually felt good, so in my mind, it was okay. Dad continued to do things to me until I was about nine years old. The pain began when he tried to penetrate me, and I was not laughing anymore. It hurt so bad, and I begged him to stop. I believed at that time it started to hurt him too, so he stopped that part of it. But he continued to try to make me laugh so he could have his way with me.

I must say it bothered me to tell anyone because it seemed like I was enjoying it. When it started to hurt even more, I finally told my mother.

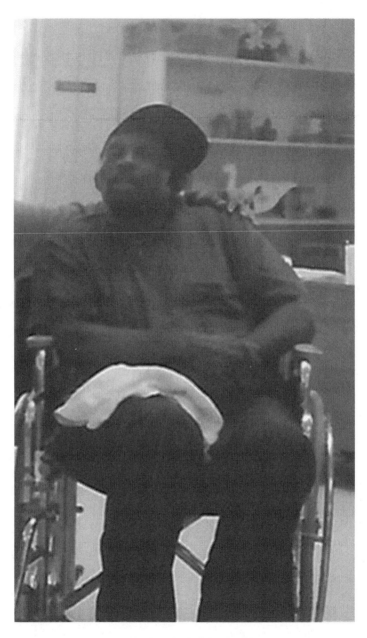

Roe Mitchell (my dad)

"What are you doing to cause this to happen to you?" asked Mother.

Well, at nine years old, I started to put it all together in my head. Since my mother asked me that question, then it must be something I was doing wrong. I said to myself that I would put on lots of clothes and stay away from Dad. That did not help. He would still come and get me out of my bed and start touching my breasts. It made them so sore that I cried and begged him to stop. This continued until I was thirteen years old when I started to fight him.

I told my mother that I was going to kill him. I started to come up with a plan.

When I told my mother, her response surprised and scared me. "Yes, if you do, I will tell the police," she said. "And they will lock you up for a long time."

At that point, I felt that I didn't have anyone to help me. I began to get mean and very bitter towards my mother because I felt that she could help me but didn't want to. She just continued to drink her liquor and would stay drunk for several days. My life kept getting worse.

I told my best friend and she said, "Girl, you need to get you a boyfriend, so he can take you away from them."

I said to myself, *maybe that will work.* So, I found this boy who was in the eleventh grade while I was in the eighth grade. We started to talk, and I told him what was happening to me at home. After talking with him for two months, he asked me to marry him, and I said "*Yes! Yes!*"

He said, "I will speak to your daddy."

I started to worry because he didn't know my father. My father was very mean, and everybody feared him. December 9th was my boyfriend's birthday. He asked my father to marry me that night. My father said, *yes,* and I could not have been happier.

Finally, I was going to leave this sick man. I did not realize at that time I was not old enough to get married, but I knew what he was doing to me was not right. On January 28, 1969, we were married and by February 1st, I was pregnant with my first child.

I talked to my husband about what I went through from when I was seven years old until I was fourteen. He promised that I would

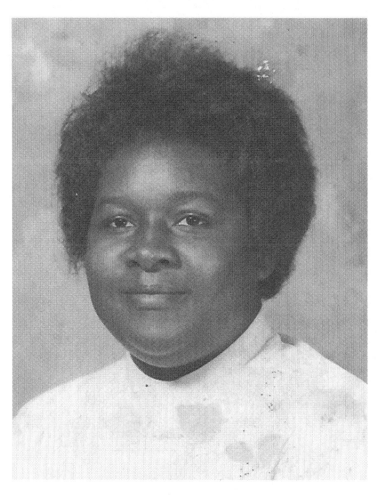

Beatress C. Lynn (me) at age 19

never hurt like that again. Well, he lied to me. Turns out, he was an abuser too. I stayed with that man for sixteen years and together we had three children. In hindsight, I feel that's all I got from that marriage: my children. During this time, I met a lady named Ms. Bell who was up in age—about sixty or seventy years old. One day, she came over to my house and said to me, "You seem very hurt. Do you want to talk about it?"

I said, "Not really."

But Ms. Bell wouldn't leave me alone, she just stood there and said, "God sent me to talk to you."

I gave her a smart look and said, "Oh really?!"

"Yes," she replied.

I scoffed. "So, talk," I retorted.

And she did. She said, "I was hurt when I was a child and it almost caused me to kill myself."

I just stood there and looked at her.

"Oh yes, and I can tell you are hurting deep inside," she told me.

She was right. I started to cry.

"It is ok," said Ms. Bell, "you don't have to talk about it now, but when you get ready, I am in the next house over. Just come to me." Then, she started to tell me her story. "I had a baby by my older brother," she confessed. "I was nine years old when he started to mess with me. He was rough with me and threatened me not to tell. He said he was going to kill me and pretend he didn't know what happened to me. So, I went along with it until I got pregnant at the age of ten years old. I had my little girl at eleven years old."

She told me how her mother kicked her out of the house and called her all kinds of names. Ms. Bell said, "When I

2 Corinthians 4:18

"While we look not at the things which are seen, but at the things not seen: for the things are seen are temporal, but the things which are not seen are eternal."

160

had my baby, I was going to get a job." She went to work with this rich, white woman, who took care of her and her baby.

By the time she got through telling her story, I broke all the way down. She took her hand, held my head up, and said, "Look at me. My girl is grown, and she is a lawyer, and she takes care of me. I don't go to my family for anything," she said. "My mother killed herself—she couldn't deal with the pain. I tried to help her, but she wanted to keep it a secret, so in a way it killed her."

I thank God for this lady because I was thinking about it too. I didn't want my children to hurt because of my life—they didn't deserve that.

Ms. Bell said, "Come see me when you want to face it."

I started to tell her my situation.

The first words that came out of Ms. Bell's mouth were, "Baby, you done nothing wrong. So, this is what I want you to focus on: forgiving yourself." She said this to me about six or seven times. She continued saying, "You were a child, and you done nothing wrong. You must forgive yourself first because you have others to forgive."

My grandchildren and me

I asked her, "Who?"

"Your mother and father," she replied.

I scoffed. "What you mean?" I asked.

She said, "You heard me."

I replied, "I done nothing to him."

She said, "I know, but this is not for them, it is for you."

Oh my God! That I just could not understand, so I asked her, "Did you forgive your brother?"

She said, "Yes and let me show you how." She went in her house, got out her old Bible and pulled a letter from it. She let me read it. She laughed and said, "That's pretty handwriting, isn't it?"

"Yes," I replied.

My daughter, talking with her grandfather
(not shown)

Ms. Bell said, "I couldn't write, so this white lady wrote it for me and sent it to my brother." The white lady told her it was just the beginning. In the letter, she wrote that whenever he was ready to talk about it to let her know. She said she knew she would meet him again one day. After about two years, she finally got a letter from her brother, and she agreed to talk to him. That's when she found out that her mother had killed herself.

Ms. Bell shared her story with me to help me kind of how that white lady helped her and gave her advice that helped her reconnect with her brother and get some closure. Therefore, I wanted to tell my story too—just like Ms. Bell. There may be someone who reads my story and may be able to get help and start the process of healing.

Eventually, I had to take my father into my home. I believe God had a hand in this because I didn't want to deal with my father, but his declining health brought us back together. No one would take him in, so I said *okay* and took him in. I remembered what Ms. Bell had told me about forgiveness, but I needed my father to admit what he had done to me.

The very next day I talked to my father about what he had done to me.

He finally broke down and said, "Yes, I did that with you. Please forgive me."

With me? What he should have said is that he did it to me! I paused for a few minutes and then I said, "I do forgive you. But I wish my mother was alive to hear you, because she accused me of lying and making all this up. She even asked me what I was doing to cause this to happen to me." I did not get a chance to forgive her, but I took care of her too. She had a stroke and was in a coma until she died. I took care of my

My daddy's sister-in-law and me in the hospital. This was Daddy's last day.

164

father for six years until he died. I was standing by his bed at Laurne Memorial Hospital where he died on January 25, 1992.

Before Daddy died, he told me what happened to him at six-years-old. My father was raised by white people. This white man would beat him and make him do things he didn't want to do. It would hurt him very badly. He said that I was the first person he ever told. He wanted me to laugh and not hurt. Again, I do believe you must be able to talk about things and get it out of your system for your own good so the healing can start. It is a long process, but you must do it.

The way I look at it is this—I said to myself, *it is not for them, it is for me.* This was the hardest thing for me to accept because I didn't do anything wrong, but I forgave him anyway.

By the time I was twenty-two, I gave my life to Christ, and He protected me. I have been living for Christ ever since. I can truly say I don't have any hate in me. I forgave my father and gave him the best care. I think it bothered him at times, but I loved him despite it all and assured him I wouldn't hurt him.

I found out that not forgiving someone doesn't hurt them, it hurts you. You are hurting yourself more by holding on to hate. Remember, I thought that some of what happened to me was my fault. There is more to this story though. I had three sisters, and I lost them all. They too had similar stories to mine. What, where, and how, are important things to ponder, but there is always more to come from knowing *why.*

YOU CAN'T HEAL UNTIL YOU FORGIVE

by Beatress C. Lynn

I tried to heal for a long time and couldn't until one day I started to reflect upon my life. I was afraid to talk about my deep hurt because of the sexual abuse I endured growing up. I always felt that I was the problem. Then one day, I realized that I was a child, and what happened to me was not my fault. I thank God for revealing that I needed to forgive myself because I wanted to get over the hurt. I even had a chance to deal directly with the person who hurt me later in life—my father. That was God's divine order for me.

One day my father had a stroke, and the doctor said that it would have been wrong for me not to take him in, so I said I would. I prayed and asked God how to handle the situation. That's when the Holy Spirit spoke to my heart and said, "Heal yourself," and that's what I did.

Having taken my father into my home, I would talk to him every day, but he didn't want to talk about what he had done to me.

My first healing question was one that had bothered him for years. "Why did you lie to my mother?" I asked.

He just looked at me for a while and finally he said, "I don't know."

"Daddy, you are not getting off that easy. Guess what? I am going to keep on asking until you tell me the truth."

To which he replied, "I was sick that's all I know."

I told him, "Don't be afraid. I won't get mad anymore, so you can talk about it. This will be between you and me."

Finally, he gave in and started to talk. I asked him why he did it, and he said that he didn't mean to hurt me. I hurt physically at first when the abuse happened, but I

167

continued to hurt emotionally for a much longer time. It affected my health too which probably is what in part led to me needing major, open-heart surgery. Fortunately, by the grace of God the surgery was successful.

I could not begin the healing without taking an important step—I needed to forgive. I do believe that healing takes time. However, if you do not deal with the root cause of the pain, there can be neither healing nor forgiveness. I am living proof that, if you trust in God, all things are possible. I am still here in my right mind even though I truly forgave my father.

I told my aunts what my dad did to me. Even though they did nothing about it, I still forgave them, and I don't have a bit of malice towards them. Since 1992, I decided I would not hurt myself anymore. If I didn't forgive myself, I knew I could not heal. Healing and forgiving myself was for me—not for those who hurt me.

I pray that my father asked God to forgive him before he died because I believe he was hurting too. I was surprised to learn that he was sexually molested as a child by his caregivers. It makes sense that, without him healing, the cycle of abuse continued through his hand. He was hurt, and so he passed that hurt down to me. Dad said that he never mentioned anything to anyone about the abuse he experienced except to me. That was the start of healing for him.

You must talk about what happened to you with someone. The truth must come out. I do believe that my dad didn't like what he had become, because he would get angry and couldn't control his temper. He was very abusive and mean. He didn't trust anyone. Everything he did was as if there was no tomorrow. Despite everything my father had done to me, I took good care of him for six years.

I pray that my quest for healing will help somebody to free themselves. You cannot live until you get to the point where you can forgive yourself for something you should not have had to deal with in the first place. God is so awesome. He can give you the strength to forgive and heal at the same time. I started praying at an early age for God to help me, and He did in all kinds of ways.

The only regret I have is that I did not get a chance to talk with my mother before she died. I still forgave her and my father. What bothered me so much about my mom is that she always said to me, "Don't be afraid to talk about anything that affects your life." She also said, "Don't let anything mess with you and hold up your progress." She said so many times to me that "people will cause you to miss your blessings." I wish she had lived by her own words, acknowledged the abuse, and defended me when she had the chance.

Ironically, my mom was also abused as a child, and she married a man that was abusive to her too. Our lives were so similar, and I saw her go through it. Some would say that I didn't learn anything, but I did. Abuse is hidden in kind words like *I will take care of you,* and *no one will ever hurt you again.* You tend to trust the abuser when these words are used because it seems as though they are sincere.

Oh my God, those words sound good when you come from an abusive family. All that I have known from my childhood was abuse, hurt, and pain. At seven years old, how would I have known what love or abuse looked like or felt like? But today, I can tell the difference. What Dad did to me felt good but hurt so badly. You see it hurt more as I got older and wiser. When I started to talk about it, that's when the lights came on. That's when I realized I was dying slowly and feeding myself the poison. And I had done so for years.

I thank God for allowing me to have a chance to spend some time with my dad. I said to him one morning, "Dad, you know what?" He looked up at me, and I said, "Dad, I am not mad anymore. I want you to forgive yourself and I am forgiving myself. You need to talk to God. He is waiting for you."

He began to cry and held his head down. Finally, he said, "I am ashamed of my actions. I don't know if He will forgive me or not."

I read him many scriptures on forgiving, healing, and peace until he died. My dad remembered one of the scriptures, Isaiah 55:6-7— "Seek the Lord while He may be found; call upon him while He is near. Let the wicked forsake his ways, and the unrighteous man his thoughts. Let him return to the Lord, that He may have compassion on him and to our God, for He will abundantly pardon."

My favorite scripture was John 4:13-14-- "Jesus said to her, 'everyone who drinks of this water will be thirsty again, but whoever drinks of the water that I will give him will never be thirsty again. The water that I will give him will become in him a spring of water welling up to eternal life." Jesus was speaking to the woman at the well.

I wanted to share my life story with you. I am so blessed. I have three children that are grown and raising their own kids. I have forgiven myself and my abuser, and with all my heart, I hope I have stopped the cycle of abuse—not just in my life but in those of others who may just so happen to read my story.

I'm Sharon Parker. The following are a few stories that I would like to share with those who choose to read them about my life experiences —hopefully for their reading enjoyment.

REMEMBERING BIRTHDAYS

By Sharon Parker

Willie James Parker was born in Jacksonville, Georgia in the year 1902. He was one of ten surviving children born to Nancy Collins Parker and Isome Parker. Willie was the eldest of the only two male children in this family. The home of these sharecroppers was shared by four mild-tempered girls and four other girls who had tempers that could ignite as quickly as a lit match. In the segregated South, education was not considered a necessity as was having available hands to pick cotton, tobacco, and peanuts. Needless to say, life was hard even in the most prosperous years of a good harvest. Without engine driven vehicles, the family traveled by horse-drawn wagons, between Georgia and Florida in pursuit of work.

As time marched on in the life of each child, the girls married—as was expected and hoped for—to relieve the burden of a mouth to feed. The two males gained work "chipping boxes," the process of using an axe to slice diagonal cuts into the bark of trees to collect the sap which eventually becomes syrup.

In early 20th century America, accusations and infractions on young black men were often not warranted and mostly false. This practice by local white authorities was in an effort to incarcerate or murder black youths, thereby holding some control over the population.

Willie and his brother worked together for several years in Georgia. It was not very long before it was their turn to have a run-in with the law. Whatever the reason was that the sheriff approached these two young men was never shared with me. However, the fact that Willie, my father, was physically holding the warrant for their arrest was proof that they were never captured. The old document became yellowed over the years but was still intact.

Willie and Harry told the sheriff he had two choices: the sheriff could return to the authorities and say he could not find the Parker brothers, or he could not return to the authorities at all. You can guess which choice the sheriff made. How my Uncle Harry continued to evade jail is unknown, but Willie had to make haste out of the South. He ventured to New York City not knowing one single soul to help him. As God would have it, he came across a young black man, Elijah Jackson, who provided a famished Willie with a large piece of cheese and turned him towards shelter. Eventually, Willie found work and began his life in a new city.

While the Parker brothers worked in their occupations, the Parker sisters grew into women who bore many children. Two of the girls were barren, but the others produced enough to share with those without any. I had thirty-two first cousins. Mostly all were raised together in the same southern community, but my sister and I were born in New York City.

Male births among the Parker sisters occurred but not nearly as often as they were produced by one sister, Deotha Parker Latimer. Deotha had two girls and seven boys; however, one boy did not survive.

I remember with fondness the many visits to New York by some of my cousins from the Latimer clan. They were in awe of the big city, and we were in awe of them.

It is not usual for the males of a family to remember and pass along family history. Most times it is the female who will share the stories, as well as the family secrets, once she determines her children can handle hearing them. As we know, many family secrets are not pleasant to hear especially among Black families who had to find ways to survive in a hostile United States.

It is particularly unusual when all the brothers in one family can remember the birth order of so many first cousins as well as those of their own siblings. This oddity of nature belongs to the Latimer brothers. From the oldest brother to the youngest, each man can quote what child was born in what year, and to what aunt. In addition to the birth of cousins, they can also tell the year each aunt and uncle passed away. Because they lived among their aunts, uncles and cousins, there were many colorful stories to tell, and they did not hold back. Our other cousins born to the sisters of Deotha, male or female, could not recite the birth order of each cousin like the Latimer brothers could. From the oldest Parker female, May Bell, to the youngest, Rachel, 25 cousins were born in the town of McRae in Telfair County, Georgia. The Latimers knew the birthdates of them all.

They told me their passion for family history came from their mother, Deotha. My Aunt Deotha apparently spoke of her nieces and nephews to her own children, giving them the sense of importance and passion to remember each family member.

Having no brothers of my own that survived, the Latimer brothers became the brothers we missed in our household to my sister and me. We held them in high esteem, and my dad trusted them to take us anywhere, knowing we would be safe. Not only were we safe with and protected by the Latimer brothers, but they never had any confrontations with each other that would turn violent. As siblings there were disagreements and disputes, but never any violence. Whenever there was a difference of opinion regarding an issue, the matter was settled over playing cards—bid whist in particular. The winner held the winning hand.

The oldest male, Nathaniel (Nate), was my hero in my youth. He was an Air Force Veteran who filled my lonely teenage years with letters from the various parts of the world he traveled. He never forgot to send me a birthday card for which I was always delighted.

After I moved to Georgia, he generously held barbecues at his home each summer holiday. He spared no expense on various meats, salads, and drinks. He loved to cook and used vegetables from his garden to experiment with creating different and wonderful meals. We had so much fun listening to old rhythm and blues music from as far back as the 1940s. Nate was also a seasoned carpenter, and many times came to the rescue of my female cousins and I when we needed work done in our homes.

Another brother, Robert, is a poet. Grateful for the generosity of our cousin Ann, who for over 30 years provided the entire family and many friends with an enormous Thanksgiving meal, Robert wrote a poem in her honor, expressing her kindness to everyone desiring to partake in the feast.

Parker Latimer was given my dad's surname as tribute to the Parker family since he and his brother, Harry, had no surviving male children. Parker, also a veteran, took the time to write letters to me during his tour in Vietnam. He enjoyed reminding me of how my birth order comes after his and just before his younger brother, Jerry. When I was sixteen years old, enjoying a weekend trip to Georgia with my cousin Robert, it was Parker Latimer who gave me my first driving lesson. I still remember the experience of driving a car for the very first time in my life down the quaint country roads. Parker said I was "a natural" and I was thrilled.

Larry, the real estate baron, allowed me to stay in his home for seven months after I arrived in Atlanta. It was there that I lived while exploring employment opportunities and learning how to maneuver around the town.

Jerry is truly the brother my mother did not birth. Family genetics is so interesting because in our youth our school pictures of us showed him and me having the exact same faces. In my young years, I often looked at that photo in the family album, wondering when I took the class photo with my hair pulled back so tightly. Then, after asking my mother when I sat for the picture, she said it was not me at all—it was my cousin Jerry.

The sisters to the Latimer brothers have become as close to me as any sister could. They have taken me under their wings and included me with their other siblings, showing me the same love and support.

We are all seniors now. Our times together have more meaning than ever as we realize that life on earth is not forever. Many of our other cousins have passed on. Remembering them with fondness has become a topic of conversation among us thanks to the Latimer brothers' unique ability to remember the most special times for family—all the birthdays.

WORKING EXPERIENCES IN GEORGIA

by Sharon Parker

When I left the North for better career opportunities in Georgia, I was confident there would be several, if not many, great possibilities awaiting me. After all, I left a well-paying supervisory staff position with the city government. The unfortunate thing about my position was that it was political and had no promise of longevity. However, I held an undergraduate degree from a city university and could boast of work experience in various Fortune 500 companies over a nineteen-year period.

Surely, there had to be a professional position within the sprawling Atlanta business community that would be perfectly suited for me. My family members, as well as others who ventured south from the North, assured me that Northerners—especially with my credentials—would be hired almost immediately.

To my disappointment, the work world in Atlanta was quite different. There were thousands of other people looking for the same thing I was and being from the North I held no badge of honor. Not only did I find it difficult getting hired, but when I finally was the favoritism enjoyed by employees who were local was hard for me to understand. In each workplace the favorite workers were allowed to be tardy and perform poorly, yet they got rewarded. I always started work early and took great pride in the excellence of work I was commissioned to perform. To see others rewarded for doing less was disturbing and disappointing.

CORPORATE AMERICA

by Sharon Parker

The first full time position I held in Atlanta was with one of the top ten best companies in the U.S.—possibly the world. I accepted an administrative support position with the expectation that I would soon move into a higher position once my professionalism, attitude, and work ethics were discovered. Coming from an environment that was not technologically advanced was certainly challenging. The company prided itself on developing employees. Well, this was their mission during my first year but that soon started to change and became as erratic as Georgia weather. At first, I was promised every tool I needed to succeed. This meant training classes in every aspect of the work we were expected to perform. However, this didn't happen in my case.

My co-worker in the neighboring workstation was assigned the task of training me to perform the fundamentals of our job. This young woman was dealing with a divorce and did not have anything other than the trials of her life on her mind. Our manager found it necessary to admonish my co-worker for practically ignoring me. I had to seek out other administrative personnel to help me get my assignments completed.

During my first year of employment, despite the lack of support, I was assigned a project that should have been directed at an employee with more experience in the company. Our manager understood this but decided to slight the worker who wanted the assignment and instead gave me the challenge. I worked hard and, with the help of others, the project was so well done that I was presented with an award for outstanding work.

By then my co-worker had been chastised several times, not only for being uncooperative with me but for errors made in the daily routine of her own desk. Had I performed as she did, there would be no question—I would have been terminated. Based on my achievements, I expected to get a better position. Instead, I watched as my co-worker was promoted to a higher position that was completely out of administrative support. Instead of a better position for me, I was transferred to a different location which was far from where I lived with no public transportation available to get there. If I had not had a vehicle, I would have lost my job with that company.

At the new distant facility, I worked next to one other support person who was hired after I was. She was old enough to have a daughter who also worked for the company but in a different location. We had the same responsibilities, but after a year, she was promoted, and I was not. My evaluations were above board. When I inquired about why a promotion was not considered for me, I was told that the other person had more years working in secretarial positions. That was not even a realistic excuse. Perhaps the fact that my co-worker's husband held a position with a major airline and secured air travel passes for the managers was the real reason. My guess is that had more to do with her getting promoted over me than her years as a secretary. Discrimination is not always a black and white thing.

ACADEMIA

by Sharon Parker

My second job was the result of an undertaking by a former United States President. It came under the umbrella of a prominent university in Atlanta. Consequently, this project carried a great deal of clout due to the sponsorship of this former President. Our location became a common meeting place for many deal makers and deal breakers of Atlanta as well as famous celebrities who often visited our site. Again, I was an administrative assistant. As exciting as it was to work there, I understood the job did not have longevity. I considered it to be a steppingstone into the Emory University system. I was given the unofficial title of Lead Secretary because of my prior experience. My performance was considered excellent.

The director had a direct secretary who came to the project with an education that did not exceed a high school diploma. She did not have any special skills and, in fact, made it clear that she had always been nothing more than a secretary and had no desire to be anything else. While I worked on the project, I submitted applications for various administrative positions at Emory to no avail.

After one year, the director's secretary was offered a permanent position within Emory. She was transferred to the Emory system while I was left to find my own way to a better job.

COUNTY GOVERNMENT

by Sharon Parker

The third employer I worked for placed me in a support position at the beginning of my time with them. It was a local government. Eventually, I was awarded a staff position that better respected my background and experience. but what I saw before that time came was truly shocking. I learned that in Atlanta, and possibly in every other major city, who you know weighs a great deal more than education, experience, and work ethics.

Before the staff position that I was eventually promoted into, I sat across from my counterpart who appeared to have an extremely close relationship with our supervisor. This developed because both experienced tragic losses of their spouses. In the case of our supervisor, the county was generous enough to grant paid time off to allow him the necessary time to get his affairs in order. When my counterpart lost her spouse, our supervisor afforded her the same consideration for which she took complete advantage.

Our supervisor took his time off all at once to leave the demands of his position to alternate personnel who could plan to expedite procedures in a timely fashion. This subordinate took advantage of the supervisor's time off by coming into work one to two hours before the end of the workday and did this quite frequently. Her reasons for tardiness, and in some cases total absenteeism, were never questioned. The employee enjoyed bragging about not having a legitimate reason for her absenteeism.

She knew she had the supervisor, "In the palm of her hand," as she boldly told other employees.

One of the responsibilities of this office was to receive and process taxpayer checks issued for various types of citations. As I was charged with handling the desk of my absent counterpart, I came across several checks in envelopes that had been overlooked for months. I brought this to the attention of our supervisor, but he was unconcerned about the oversight. After a year of this type of office conduct, the supervisor considered this absent employee for a management seat. However, she left the job to pursue her own private ambitions.

Another observation of blatant favoritism was an employee who just could not or preferred not to make a full week at work. The employee moved to our work site from an area that was quite a distance away. Consequently, fighting traffic from such a long distance was harrowing for this clerk. In this situation, the clerk rarely completed a full week at work and continued this behavior for several years until retirement.

Another observance of preferential treatment was demonstrated in the Pension Division. The veteran professional in this position worked up pension calculations for those eligible to retire after a thirty-year stay with the county. This employee's efficiency was excellent, and the results of the calculations never needed to be questioned.

Upon the pension administrator's retirement, a new person was hired by arrangement of a top executive to fill the position. The new employee had worked with the executive in a prior office setting. I must think this executive did not feel that very much effort was required to learn and perform the tasks of this job. The position paid well over $50,000 annually, and the friend started at this rate of pay.

A clerk worked under the pension administrator who was second in line for processing all the particulars of pensions along with health benefits and life insurance. The job of the administrator was to meet with each eligible employee and explain that person's pension payment. The clerk only had to process the paperwork. However, there was a glitch in this process. Anyone calling the new administrator for information was referred, by the voice mail system, to call the clerk. There were not many more than a few questions about pensions that the administrator could answer. It was not until two years later that the administrator was finally asked to resign.

In the Budget Department an analyst made a two-million-dollar error. Ultimately, funds were moved from other accounts to replace the shortfall. There was no reprimand of the analyst. One other analyst moved around funds without proper approval from the Board of Commissioners. My responsibility was to monitor funding and the redistribution of funds, and had I not caught the error I would have been severely corrected. This analyst did not receive as much as a scolding.

As soon as it was determined that a reduction in the workforce would help the county's deficit, offers to qualifying employees came out. Fortunately, I was among those who qualified, and I accepted the offer. I gratefully retired from the circus of misappropriation of funds, favoritism, and unethical workplace practices.

THE SHORTCUT HOME

by Sharon Parker

It was the end of summer in 1985. I was the proud mom of a son who was about to begin his first semester at college in upstate New York. The dream of seeing your child off to college was no small miracle in my opinion. Although the drive would be four hours long, I was happy to be doing it. My prayers to God that my child would want to attend an institution of higher learning were answered. While his schoolmates and childhood friends were not motivated to take this journey, he was committed to walking a greater path.

Throughout the years of raising my son, a small still voice repeated to me, "Just keep the faith." His motivation to pursue higher learning was mostly due to the influences of uncles, aunts, and cousins who had achieved college degrees. He also remembered the years of his early life when I had to leave him in the hands of his grandparents and other sitters while I pursued my own college education. My son also found and stood steadfast in his relationship with God.

It was our second trip to the school, the first having happened earlier in the summer for orientation. This time I was leaving my only child to live on his own far away from home. I struggled to keep the thought of his empty bedroom back home out of my mind.

It was a lovely drive into Manhattan. We traveled across bridges and into the mountains and hills of upstate New York. The highways eventually began to dip up and down giving challenge to my small sedan with a standard transmission. How pleasantly different the atmosphere was there. The concrete sidewalks and tall buildings of the city were soon replaced with green lawns and sprawling two-story and ranch homes. Many had barns and sheds tucked behind front entrances that stood at the end of long winding driveways.

After getting stopped by a highway state trooper with a warning for speeding, we finally arrived at the school. Parents and students mingled with faculty. Discussions about that place—far from home—and what to expect in the coming winter months was the topic of everyone's conversation. I was happy to meet a parent—a mom—also from the city, who was there with her daughter. Her anxiety about leaving her child mirrored mine. I was happy to have a parent with the same ideals and hopes for her child as I did and was especially glad when she told me about a shortcut back to the city. I did not think she had ill intentions towards me, as I believed what she told me. Her route was sure to cut off at least one and a half hours of travel time from this four-hour commute. I was excited.

Unfortunately, I neglected to write down the instructions the lady gave me that seemed so simple at the time. This was the mid-1980s and cell phones and GPS technology were not yet available for the general population. The route, as she relayed it to me, was no more than a few turns up the highway while traveling in the opposite direction from the way I came.

After spending the last hours of our visit saying goodbye and offering all avenues of advice to our children, I headed out for home. That time, I drove along the highway, using the alternative route offered by my new friend. It was evening and the sun had about two hours remaining before it would go down.

I drove west instead of east and chased the sun as it was setting, looking for Highway 336 as instructed. On and on I drove without seeing the signage. The quaint homes dotting each side of the highway became fewer and fewer as vast areas of farmland engulfed them. Suddenly, they didn't have as much appeal to me as when I began my trip from the city. I needed to find the right highway.

Finally, I decided that by turning left on any highway I came across, I would be travelling in a southern direction and therefore getting closer to the city. At the first sign of a public place, I stopped to inquire of my whereabouts. It was a bar that was populated with middle-aged white men who eyed me as though I was from outer space. I had to stop there since it was the only place with people in it that I'd seen since I left the campus. I'd been driving for several hours and discovered that I was in Corning, New York, more than a hundred miles from Morrisville. I could only pray that someone there would know where Highway 336 was and be kind enough to tell me how to get to it. However, I was out of luck. The bartender was not very much help and he had no idea where I'd find a highway leading back to New York City. I left this bar quickly and prayed I would not be followed by any of those men who might have ill intentions. I just travelled on.

By that time, nightfall had come, I was no closer to any sign that would show me a southern route. Finally, I made another left turn and I drove. Before long, I was in farmland where the only lights I saw, serving as night lights, were those on the front porches of homes spread far apart from each other. Then, I came upon an opportunity to make yet another left turn which I did. From there, I drove to a road that only offered yet another left turn. It wasn't long before I realized I was driving around in a circle.

By then, I was three hours into the trip and a very long way from home. Getting lost was not my only dilemma. Early the next morning, my agenda was to get to the bank to send the school money for my son's tuition, then to the post office to send it off, pick up my packed suitcase, and be on time to catch a flight to Atlanta, all before 10:00 a.m. How was I to do all that when I was still in upstate New York, hours from the city and lost? As I slumped deeper into despair, I remembered how in many other dangerous situations in my life, prayer to my savior miraculously brought me through the storms. It was at that moment that I loudly called out to Him. "Jesus, please help me!" I cried out.

After calling on the Lord, I looked into my rearview mirror and instantly saw a pair of headlights in the distance coming towards me. It was the only other vehicle on the road besides my own. My heart began to race. I knew how dangerous it was to trust strangers—especially ones found in the dark of night on a lonely dirt road in an unfamiliar area. I felt the blood rush to my face. The driver stopped at the stop sign where I was located. His face showed confusion and I am sure he was surprised to see another vehicle in this deserted place. I felt I had to take a chance. I jumped from my car to get his attention. God be with me I prayed, and I was not ignored.

The other driver was a young white man, and he was curious and amazed that me, a young black woman, was driving out in that desolate country, in the dark, and apparently very far from her desired destination. He asked me how I even found the place I was at. He was friendly. By the grace of God, this young man was on his way to Pennsylvania after tending to a farm he ran in upstate New York. He not only got me onto the highway by allowing me to follow him but purchased my coffee at our gas stop and paid for my toll at the bridge that would get me back to the city.

Finally, I made it back to my apartment in Queens, New York. Even without having slept for many hours, that morning I was able to fulfil all my commitments, as well as make my flight to Atlanta. That adventure reminded me to not be so trusting of what others might tell you without seeing proof of what they are saying. Again, the Lord got me out of a serious situation, and I believe the experience was to use me to give testimony to others about having faith in Him.

Dorothy Kinsey

MY JOURNAL UNFINISHED

by Dorothy Kinsey

Sharing Her Poems

Can you imagine turning fifty years old and not knowing how you got there? You may have remembered but I didn't. The morning of my birthday, I lay in bed and thought, "What am I going to do today? Well, let's see. I think I might just go out and buy me a journal." Since I left my forties falling in and out of love and being depressed and lonely, I thought to myself *how bad can my fifties be? Sixties? Seventies? How bad?*

With pencil and paper in hand, I was about to start writing in the journal. The plan was to write about my day-to-day journey in life. I am going to get a little off the subject and bring up something my mother asked me.

Mother asked, "Dot, what are you going to do after you graduate from high school?"

I replied, "I am going to be a nurse."

Mom looked at me with a smile and said, "God can change that." She killed my spirit.

Let's go back to my journal. When I was about to put my thoughts on paper, the Lord took control. The thoughts were not from my mind, they were from my soul. These are the words as follows:

Father, I am very lonely. My body longs
for companionship. But my mind thinks not.

What has become of me? When any ray of
light is overcome by darkness (fear),
I feel myself falling into nothingness.
I pray, Heavenly Father, stay with me.
Amen

I was so embarrassed. I thought, *I wrote that? Oh no!* You
may ask, *did you ever get out of that loneliness?* Not really.
When you deal with loneliness, one has a habit of
dreaming.

See these words in the poems on the following pages...

THE LOVE OF MY DREAMS

by Dorothy Kinsey

When my thoughts have excused themselves
from my inner being out through my pen, my heart
will dictate its words of my unforeseen love.

When my many past dreams foretold of my future love
My mind has hidden them in the shadows.

Sometimes my loneliness will overpower my serenity.
But my spirit secretly searches for my promised love.

For within the shadows, my heart has waited.
You, my love, came alone and rescued it.

Our spirits are one. They have locked.
This may not be of our choosing.

It may be the choice of the Great Creator.

Okay falling in and out of love. Maybe I fell in love a couple
of times. I think.

These were my secret endeavors. These poems are from the
heart. Look and see...

A LOVE LETTER TO SOMEBODY

by Dorothy Kinsey

The first time I saw you,
I knew you were someone special.
But my fear of love left me silent.
Oh Lord, when will this fear end?

When you spoke my name,
my heart skipped a beat.
Oh, my poor heart.

When I speak your name, my tongue swells.
My words, I fear, are incoherent.
My love for you, I cannot speak of.

I can only think of you.
I can only dream of you.
I can write about my love for you.

I can share these words of love to the world.
However, my words are only meant for you.
From someone who loves you.

LOVER UNKNOWN

by Dorothy Kinsey

I missed your call today.
You never called.

I missed the touch of your hands
as they caress my body.
You never touched me.

I missed the warmth of your lips
as they touched mine.
You never kissed me.

I missed the passionate love we made.
We never made love.

I missed the sound of your voice
when you called my name.
You don't know my name.

Oh! What a fantasy world I live in.
My unknown lover.

IT'S NOT FAIR

by Dorothy Kinsey

It is not fair
at this time in my life
I meet you.

Why could I have not met you
in the beginning?
It is not fair.

My heart ran off. Betrayed me,
falls in love with you.
It is just not fair.

My heart has left my mind
to defend itself from the—what ifs.

As my mind sinks into chaos,
this feeling that I have
is devouring every part of my inner being

Tell me my love, what am I to do?
When my will to fight has failed me?
It is just not fair.

When my premonition of the future
is telling me to surrender.
Your mind will lose.

This feeling of love will win.
It is just not fair!

Now this is where depression sets in:

A SONG OF GRIEF

by Dorothy Kinsey

The grief that I have weighs heavy on my soul.
Its weight is like that of a thousand-pound anvil.

I feel my strength is failing. I can't go on.
Please help me, Master.

My heart is broken into so many pieces, Father.
I fear it cannot be put back together again.

Please help me, Father.
I know you have the power.

My mind is in chaos, oh Lord.
Thinking rationally has become impossible.

I dread facing another day.
I can no longer see the sunrise or the sunset.
The tears cloud my eyes.

I know my tears, like the rain, will subside.
The sun will shine through.
That's how the Master works

Throughout all my trials tribulations,
the Master will stay with me

As for me, being a true and faithful servant.
I will wait.

ABYSS

by Dorothy Kinsey

Father, please remove me from this abyss.

The emptiness that I feel has overpowered me.

Like the storms threaten sea
my soul has become restless.

The pain of heartbreak has fallen upon me.

I know not why.
I have not lost a love at this time.

But yet the tears form in the well of my eyes.

Lord, am I to cry now for a love
that is promised in the future?

My Lord, has the restless soul
of another become mine?

Is this his pain of heartbreak that I feel?
Has his soul become empty?

Is it his cries that I hear as I silently pray to you?

I wish he knew of you
Lord and the peace you can bring.

Then I must continue to pray, Heavenly Father.
Please Lord, remove him and me from this abyss

Bitter—I did not mention bitter:

THE GAMES WE PLAY

by Dorothy Kinsey

It was her game
You was her king
She was your queen

She held the ace of spade.
You was cut. You lost.

It was his game.
He was my king.
I was his queen.

He held the ace of spades.
I was cut. I lost.

This is our game
You are my king.
You hold the ace of spades.
I will not be cut.

On the contrary, my dear,
Ha, this is my game.
I am the joker.
The joker is wild.

This is not the end of my journal, but I will end it today. However, all thanks go to my Heavenly Father for allowing me to share with you.

A CHILD'S STRUGGLE FOR EDUCATION

by Dr. Ingrid J. Benjamin, Ph.D., LSC CCHT

This is the memoir of a little girl who fought and made tremendous sacrifices to obtain an education while living in the ghetto with her grandmother. It was her dream that when she grew up, her life would be different.

This is a small part of my story. It is neither the beginning nor the end. This is a true story of my childhood struggles to get an education while growing up in Guyana on the South American continent. These struggles, however, are not typical of every Guyanese since we were all raised under different circumstances and socio-economic factors. The education system in Guyana was different from that in the United States. Some of the names of the protagonists in my story were changed to protect their anonymity.

After my grandmother took me from my mother when I was about eight years old, we went to live in New Amsterdam where she enrolled me in Mission Chapel School, which was named after the church next door. This primary school—or elementary school as Americans would call it—was very good for me. I met the most amazing educators there. They were all interested in their students' wellbeing and success. I spent a few weeks in *Standard 2*, which is the equivalent of *second grade* in the USA, and then I was transferred to *Standard 3* where I remained for the duration of the school year.

Academics were no problem for me. I received many awards for my grades and good conduct. Standards 4 - 5 were around the point at which most students wrote the national exam called the *Common Entrance Exam* to enter secondary school or high school. A good grade on that exam would ensure a scholarship and acceptance into one of the top high schools in the country. There were other high schools that accepted lower grades. Only a chosen, special few students were given the opportunity to take this exam and be awarded scholarships to go to top ranked high schools free of charge.

Although a scholarship to high school meant the tuition was free, parents were still responsible for purchasing school uniforms and textbooks. I was not so fortunate to be selected to write this exam—even with my excellent grades and awards. I did not know or understand what the criterion for the selection process was. I do know that many of the students who went to the top high schools came from the higher echelon in the community and many parents paid the high tuition for their children. Everyone just accepted it as the norm, and I had to pursue a more difficult path.

After Standard 6, one would think that, according to the natural progression of classes, the next stage would be Standard 7. However, there was no Standard 7. The next class was Form 1. This continued up to Form 6. Most students left school between Forms 4 and 5. Form 1 marked the beginning of high school while the end of high school was between Forms 5 and 6. A student could have spent between seven and eight years in primary school and four to six years in high school. Nursery school was not a requirement. A student could have left high school as early as age sixteen having completed the required courses and taken the General Certificate Exam.

I continued until I got to Standard 6 where I was allowed to take other national exams that were less recognized. The first exam was the *Preliminary Certificate Exam (PC)*. A passing grade in that exam allowed you to get into a lesser known or recognized high school. Then the *College of Preceptors Exam (CP)* allowed students to write individual subjects such as arithmetic, geometry, and English. That was also another path to high school which gave students between the ages of 16 and 18 the option to further their education by applying for training as an assistant teacher or nurse or find other employment. A passing grade would also allow a student to attend the Technical Institute. This marked the end of a student's life at the elementary level.

Students also had another choice for their academic career which was to go to secondary school or high school. There was no minimum or maximum age requirement to attend or leave elementary or high school nor was there an age requirement to take the PC or CP exams. Attendance at high school was not a requirement. Many students did not attend, mainly because of the high cost of tuition. Also, students had other choices after leaving elementary school, including trade school, technical institute, work, apprenticeship, or commercial school. This system may seem very confusing or archaic, but it worked perfectly for me.

The education system today has been changed to one that is more inclusive. Every child now has an equal opportunity to take the *Common Entrance Exam* to enter high school regardless of their socio-economic background. Even though the high schools are still ranked, each child has the same privilege to attend high school, according to a point value system, coupled with the average points received on the exam. All government-controlled institutions, from elementary school to university were tuition free by the time I exited high school.

I passed both the PC and CP exams by the time I was fourteen. However, regardless of my situation, I wanted to go to high school where I could take the *General Certificate Examination*, Ordinary or Advanced levels. These exams were sent from England. It was equivalent to a high school diploma here in the U.S. Students were required to pass with good grades, As or Bs, along with completing five subjects at one sitting, including English and math, or seven or more subjects at two sittings. After high school, students also had the opportunity to either go to Teachers' College or the University of Guyana or land a decent job in public service or the private sector. Alphabetical grades were not given in the regular school exams. Instead, students were given a numerical grade and ranked according to the grades received.

At the elementary school level, the older girls went to the home economics center once a week to learn various house-keeping skills while the boys went to woodworking to learn carpentry. Some of the teachers prepared students to take national exams by offering free lessons. This tutoring took place in the afternoons after school and sometimes on the weekends. Some teachers even opened their homes to some of us for extra classes on the weekends, including Sundays, without charging a fee. If a lot of students were going to be present on the weekends, then classes were held in school instead of in a teacher's home. I was always present whenever and wherever classes were offered. All my teachers did an excellent job at teaching and preparing us to take these exams.

This brings me to an ingenious way in which I got my education as a child. I had no mother and father to support my efforts. I only had an old, hardworking grandmother. It was imperative for me to make my mark in this world. One day, as I was playing under the stoop, I saw my friend, Jacqueline, looking down at me from her window. She lived in the neighboring yard. I invited her to play but she said that she could not come downstairs to play with me. Almost immediately, something happened to me. I cannot explain to this day what it was. But I picked up my bag of toys, went upstairs, threw them in the corner, and sat down all alone. I felt rage, disappointment, anger, confusion, and rejection once again. Maybe it was the way that Jacqueline spoke to me. I did not think that anyone could experience all these emotions at the same time, but I certainly did.

As I sat there in my bewilderment, I thought to myself, *why doesn't anybody like me?* By that time, I had experienced so much rejection that I did not know what to do with myself. My mother treated me differently from the rest of her children. My father, who preferred to visit my godmother, passed by my home and only came to see me once. My dark skin seemed to be a repellant whenever my sister and I were out in public. Many adults would gravitate towards her because of her fair complexion. I would be left standing there as though I were invisible.

My god sisters often said to me, "Ingrid is going to punish," but never gave me an explanation for what that meant. My Sunday school teacher did not want her granddaughter to speak to me even though I did nothing wrong—I was just a child growing up in the ghetto. The one thing I knew for sure was that I had to do better. I had to carve out a better life for myself—one in which I would be respected and not feel rejected, dejected, and alone. I was not going to live in the ghetto, "nigger yard," tenement yard, or whatever derogatory terminology was used to describe the place where I grew up.

A tenement yard is similar to a plantation style compound in the United States. There were several little houses, consisting of three rooms—a kitchen, living room, and bedroom. A family of two or more people lived in each house. There were also outhouses and one community bathroom along with one standpipe in the yard for everyone to use. There was no running water in the houses. All the houses and amenities were in one small area in the yard. This style of living was also referred to as a "nigger yard." I do not know the history behind this name.

I remembered what Mama kept saying to me, "Get an education, then you would not have to depend on no man for nothing." She said this to me over and over again. I wondered why she was saying this to me. After all, I was only a child. At that point, my mind wandered to my own surroundings. The women in our yard did not have an education, and the men—whether working or not—took full advantage of them. They physically abused them daily to the point of hospitalization and deformity. I do not know if there were any laws that protected women from abuse at that time. All I knew was that some of the women would be absent for a few days, and when they reappeared, they were in bandages and walking crooked.

There were endless fights and colorful cussing matches—sometimes all day long. The police came regularly. I guess they were accustomed to it. They knew my neighbors by name and could predict who started the fight. After a while, they did not make any arrests, they just talked to the perpetrators and left. Then, there would be peace and quiet for a little while—perhaps, four or five hours. After that though, the saga continued again like a sequel in a soap opera.

Many young women left elementary school and started working the streets. Some of them got pregnant and bore children out of wedlock while some got abortions. Whatever the situation was, they continued in the tradition of ghetto living. There were no betrothals or weddings there. Men and women just "shacked up."

On the other hand, I was exposed to another way of life. I visited rich people's homes, either when my grandmother worked there or with my god sisters on Sunday afternoons after Sunday school. I also went camping with other children from a higher socio-economic background. My grandmother taught me how to eat with knives and forks, how to set a table, and how to sit and eat the correct way. She taught me good etiquette, table manners, and how to conduct myself in public or, as she would say, "among people." People were impressed everywhere I went. That was the life I wanted for myself. It was my destiny, and I was going to pursue it. I simply abhorred ghetto living.

When my grandmother, who I called Mama, came home one evening, I told her that I wanted to go to commercial school in the afternoons after school. I thought that would be my passport out of the ghetto. The school taught Pitman's English, typewriting, and shorthand. It prepared young men and mostly young women to work in a business setting, doing mainly secretarial work. Mama said alright without giving it a second thought and she said that she would talk to Aunt Maggie, who was the owner of the school the following day. Aunt Maggie, as she was fondly called, had prepared many young women and a few men to be successful secretaries and clerks in offices. As a matter of fact, she was the best in her training and profession.

I had already figured out how I would pay for that school. My Uncle Andy, Mama's son, sent money to her every week. I would save my allowance, which we called a pocket piece, every week in an empty Ovaltine or Milo can—whichever one was available. Then, when we sold eggs—Mama and my younger sister Carol reared chickens under the house—I would save some of that money too and leave the rest to buy food for the chickens and us. If any money was left over from the market on Saturdays, I would put that in the can as well. That was my great financial plan, and it worked.

I was about eleven years old when I started Pitman's Commercial School in the afternoons, while I attended elementary school during the day. Sometimes I had to stay after school with the other students for tutoring before I went to commercial school. Thanks to my plan, there was always money for my tuition, and some left over.

Meanwhile, as I continued to grow, I needed nice clothes like the other girls. Mama could not afford to buy "ready- made" clothes for us. One day I loosened one of my old dresses to see how it was sewn together. Then, I went to the fabric store and asked the sales lady how much cloth I needed to make a dress. She told me, and I bought the cheapest cotton, three yards for $1. I went home and cut my dress out, using the old dress as a pattern—a little bigger, of course. I sewed it on my grandmother's old sewing machine, and it worked. This was the beginning of my dressmaking career. My grandmother no longer had to pay a dressmaker to get my clothes sewn. I used that money to make my own dresses. I could even buy shoes and socks. I saved anything that was left over.

My neighbor, Mr. James, who lived in the front house, remarried after the death of his wife. His new wife, Ms. Irene, was a dressmaker. I went over to help her on Friday afternoons and some Saturdays to hem and baste clothes for her customers. She showed me how to measure and cut dresses the correct way without using patterns. I loved to sew and dress up, but I did not want to make it my career.

I sewed all my clothes—even my grandmother's. When I learned to do smocking—special embroidery stitches—in school, I smocked some of my dresses and blouses. Everyone loved my smocked clothes. My aunt's friend brought some white satin material and Coats thread and asked me to smock a dress for her baby's christening. Not only did I smock the baby's dress, I sewed it with beautiful, puffed sleeves. I also made the baby a little bonnet.

When Ms. Jenn came to pick up the dress, she was surprised, almost going into instant shock to see her baby's dress. I can still remember seeing her lifting the dress up and turning it around as she touched the smocked areas. She kept asking, "Did you do this by yourself, Buggie?" She told me, "It's so clean and beautiful." It was a picturesque, long flowing, white satin dress with white smocking around the neck and the end of the short-puffed sleeves. I did the scalloped lace trim around the top of the neck, at the end of the sleeves, and along the dress hem. I made the bonnet with the remaining white satin material, and some leftover white lace I had on hand. The lace was trimmed around the brim of the bonnet and a beautiful bow was made to tie under the baby's chin. Ms. Jenn gave me $20. This was my biggest pay day so far.

Later, as my skills improved, I made dresses for brides and bridesmaids. I also made curtains, chair covers, finger and dish towels, cushions, sheets, and pillowcases, as well as costumes. I even tried making a bathing suit. Later, when I left Guyana, I learned to use patterns, such as Vogue, to make my dresses.

I stopped sewing because of several reasons though. Some of my clients did not want to pay, some underpaid me, and of course, the most important part was my education. I went back to school to work on my BS degree and more. Also, I was very active in church work. To this day, whenever I see a beautiful dress, I not only admire it, but I also think about the type of cut, material, seams, waistline, hem line, and how the pieces were put together. I look at beautiful dresses in nostalgia and sometimes wish I had continued sewing.

One day, my mother showed up with her sewing machine to exchange it for my grandmother's machine. She said that her machine was too heavy, and it hurt her chest whenever she used it. It was an almost new machine, so we made an exchange. Several months later she returned to get her machine without Mama's machine. I told her that she needed to return Mama's machine because she could not leave our house without a sewing machine, and that I needed to use it. She said nothing and left. A few hours later, I heard a knock on the door. When I opened the door, she was standing there with a policeman. She told him that I had her sewing machine. Mama said nothing—she just sat there and rolled her eyes, as she often did whenever something was out of order. Mama and the policeman told me to give it to her. I did so. When they left, I cried and cried because I loved to sew and, at that point, I had no sewing machine.

To this day, I cannot believe that a mother would do that to her child. Moreover, to call a policeman on her twelve-year-old child who had done nothing wrong was incomprehensible. I continued to sew, but I had to do everything by hand. I learned to do different types of stitches in my sewing classes at school since I had to utilize that skill without a machine. This was a slow and daunting process. We could not afford to buy another sewing machine at the time, but a few months later, my Uncle Andy bought me another sewing machine.

I was reminded that my mother repeated this action several years later. I was away in college when my mother returned to exchange sewing machines again. My grandmother allowed her to take my sewing machine while she left hers. When I came home from college my sewing machine was gone and my mother came asking for her sewing machine once again. I promptly asked her to return mine first. She once again left and showed up a few hours later with a policeman. Guess what? History just repeated itself all over again. I gave it to her in the name of peace. A few months later, I bought another sewing machine. This time it was not portable. I also let her know that if it was removed from Mama's house for any reason, the tables would be turned, and I did not care what the outcome would be. I was very angry. I do not know how a parent could be so unfair and selfish. God knows, I cannot write what I was thinking at that time, so I will leave it alone.

Back to my money-making efforts. I joined the School Thrift Society at school. Students were allowed to save money weekly. Each student had a savings book where their savings were recorded. The teacher in charge of the School Thrift Society also kept their own records of our savings. Some of us students even raised funds on Fridays by making homemade ice cream and cakes. We had one and a half hours for lunch, so we had adequate time to prepare our snacks. We shared the money equally and saved it in the School Thrift Society. We could not access this money until we left school. Some students left with hundreds of dollars. I only had about $100 because I had other things I needed to do with my money.

My hard, nappy hair was beginning to be a problem. Whenever my aunt washed my hair, she yanked it so hard I would be screaming. She did not stop or even pause until she was finished washing, drying, and combing my hair. We did not have a hair dryer, so even drying it with a towel made my head hurt. Mama eventually sent me to a hairdresser, Madam Thom, to get it washed and pressed.

I could only go on Saturdays to get my hair done after I was finished with my chores, which included going to the market, washing clothes, hanging them on the line to dry, house cleaning, scrubbing the stairs, and sometimes cooking. Most of the women got their hair done on Saturdays too. By the time I got to the hair salon, it was filled with waiting patrons. I had to wait a long time to get my hair done.

Madam Thom also trained young women to become hairdressers. While I was waiting to get my hair done, I was observing and taking in everything. After all, I had nothing else to do. During Christmas and other holidays, the salon was unusually full. There were not enough "hands" to go around.

One day, I was feeling very bored. So, I asked Madam Thom if I could help her wash and dry some heads.

"You sure, Buggie?" she asked.

"Yes ma'am," I replied.

Madam Thom observed as I washed and set my first head of hair. She asked me, "Where did you learn to do this?"

I replied, "Right here, ma'am."

She said, "That's good." She allowed me to do a second and third head and so on.

One day in the salon, a lady wanted her hair pressed in a hurry and no one was available, so I asked, "Can I do it?"

Madam Thom looked at me as though I were a crazy child who was about to get her in trouble.

I said, "I'll show you." The lady quietly entrusted her head in the hands of mine—an amateur practitioner and a child to add insult to injury. It was probably not a smart move, but I was thankful for the opportunity. I started very bravely and repeated every word that I had heard Madam Thom say to her trainees. She just stood there with a dumbfounded look as I demonstrated my skills. I performed perfectly, and it was the beginning of another career—hairdressing.

When I was not dressmaking with Ms. Irene, I went to Madam Thom to be a hairdresser. My hairdressing skills came in useful later when I attended college. I made a good living, doing hair for students and friends. At that point I did not want a career in hairdressing. I was just a very curious, enterprising child.

Back to Aunt Maggie's school. I went to classes from Monday to Thursday. I learned Pitman's Shorthand, typing, and English. I did that for one year; however, no one paid much attention to me. I was the youngest student attending and the classes were large. They were not taught in conventional groups. Each student was at a different point in the textbooks, therefore we all required individual attention. Much of what I learned was self-taught. My work was corrected by one of the teachers, who spent a few minutes teaching me individually, as she did with other students. They just couldn't spend much time helping individuals.

One afternoon, my grandmother asked me if Aunt Maggie would allow me to take any exams. I told her, *no*. Then Mama told me that I would not be going back to that school. Imagine my horror when I heard that. I thought I would just take my last breath and die. I stood there dumbfounded and looked at her, but I dared not say a word. She seemed very angry.

After a long pause, she said, "I will talk to Teacher Aileen tomorrow." My grandmother was not gifted with many words. She got straight to the point and then right to the end.

I felt an immediate rush of relief. Teacher Aileen had another commercial school and had also been trained by Aunt Maggie.

When school reopened in September, I went to Victoria Commercial School. Once again, I was the youngest in attendance. The classes there were smaller, so I got more teacher-student attention. The structure was the same as Aunt Maggie's though. By the end of the second semester in March, I was preparing to take exams in elementary English and typing, as well as Theory Stage 1 Shorthand.

The older girls, who knew the system, rented all the typewriters early. I told Mama what happened, and she took me to Mr. Mendoza's shop. He repaired and sold old typewriters. I examined most of the typewriters until I found the one that I liked. I could see that Mr. Mendoza was getting impatient as he wondered what I was up to. He told my grandmother that I was very inquisitive. That did not bother me though. After all, my grandmother was paying for it, and it was my job to get her money's worth. I selected an Olympian typewriter, and it was fine. Right after, I went to my Milo money can and got enough money to pay for my exams.

Later, I learned that Mama had taken almost all her money out of the bank to purchase my typewriter. This confirmed what I already knew—she loved and cared for me even though she never told me. I knew that it was my job to work hard to make her feel proud of me. I studied, wrote, and passed all my exams. Mama did not say anything—neither did she show any emotion, but I knew that she cared anyway.

As a child, I never got hugs and kisses or any verbal encouragement, praises, or affirmations. However, when I needed anything, I always got it. You could not tell that I was from the ghetto if you did not know me. I presented myself differently by my speech, my mannerisms, and my general appearance. My grandmother did not accept anything less from me. She always insisted that I do everything to the best of my ability. For example, when the other kids were allowed to run and play in the yard barefoot, I had to wear my "yard shoes." And I had to use my house slippers in the house. Even now, I think my feet are still softer than my hands.

I was very serious about my schoolwork and showed a lot of interest in every class. Teacher Aileen always used me as an example when she wanted to make the point of being a conscientious student to the older girls. She referred to me as "this little girl."

One day when she made her usual remarks about me being a little girl, she got on my nerves, and I said so.

"That's getting me on my last nerves," I mumbled under my breath. "I am not a little girl."

Teacher Aileen actually heard me, and then changed it to, "this big girl."

I knew I couldn't win, so I left it alone.

There were three semesters in one school year. I wrote and passed all my exams. By the end of the school year, I achieved many academic awards including *Proficiency in Typewriting*. I attended the same school the following year with continued success. By the time I was fourteen, I had Pitman's Elementary, Intermediate, and Advanced Typing and English. My typing speed was 92 words per minute. My shorthand speed was 120 words per minute. This was quite an accomplishment for a fourteen-year-old.

Even though I was a smart, enterprising child, one would think that my family would be proud of me, but that was never the case. When my aunt learned that I was going to commercial school, she became very vindictive.

She told my grandmother, "You do not waste money on other people's children." She told my mother that Mama was wasting her money on me, and that I would be ungrateful.

My mother agreed with her and was very angry too. She even stopped sending me her occasional packages of clothing. I did not care because the clothes did not fit well anyway—I had to alter them to suit my taste. Mama told me to just ignore them and that they never wanted to learn anything when they were children. She told me stories about them growing up. My mother started piano lessons when she was a child and quit soon after. My aunt and one uncle did nothing but fight with other students almost on a daily basis. The only one who did something with his life was my youngest uncle who went to commercial school and later opened his own commercial school when he got married and moved to the Essequibo Coast. My other uncle attended trade school after he left school.

My aunt gave me more chores to do every day. When I did not do them to her specifications, she would hit me with sticks, pot spoons, and rolling pins—anything that she got her hands on, and when all else failed, she pulled my hair. To this day I have marks on my skin and pain in the center of my head as a result of her abuse. Many times, when she got enraged, I would run to the backyard, jump over the trench, and hide in the cemetery until she left, or Mama came home. Sometimes I would be there for several hours. Thankfully, there were many fruit trees, including coconuts, tamarind, mangoes, and jamoon, and there was lots of shade out there. I climbed the trees and got my full supply of fruits.

I used to play in the cemetery with some of the children in the neighborhood when I was much younger. We used to climb the trees and pick the fruits. We left a cutlass there so it would be convenient for us to cut coconuts and wood to make a fire for our "bush cook," a type of cookout. We took ingredients from our parents' and guardians' homes along with old pots, pans, plates, and spoons to make up our desired cuisine for the day. Those dishes were delicious. We cooked them ourselves, and they had a nice smoky flavor.

Whenever I ran out of the house, my aunt thought that I was going to the duplex at the back of the yard, and that I would become a whore. She told my uncle, and he left his home in Mackenzie, traveling for several hours just to come to Mama's house and beat me. My aunt never came to look for me. If she did, she would have known that I was not there, but hiding in the cemetery instead. Mama told me not to go to the house in the backyard, so I never went there. I had a special tomb in the cemetery that I sat on to read whenever I could grab a book on my way out. This happened at least once every couple of weeks.

My aunt made life very difficult for me. I could not do my homework or study early in the evening, so I went to bed early. There was too much noise and ruckus in the house, but somehow, I managed to get some sleep. I woke up in the wee hours of the mornings, about one to two o'clock when it was nice and quiet to study and do my homework. I was determined that nothing or no one would get in the way of my success. I was not going to allow anyone to put out the little flicker of my candlelight. I was determined to push through until I achieved my goals. I absolutely refused to allow anyone to bulldoze my plans or use a wrecking ball to destroy my future because of their ignorance or jealousy.

Even though an educational achievement should be celebrated, rewarded, and at the very least announced, I could not let my aunt or mother know of any of my own achievements for fear of their harsh reprisal. I just kept it all to myself. Only my grandmother knew of my success.

My aunt was not always indifferent towards me. I remembered being with her around the age of five. She took good care of me then. The only problem I had with her was when she washed my hair. She became very abusive when she learned that I was going to attend commercial school. I believe that she wanted me to continue in the family tradition of being domestic servants or maids and struggling in the ghetto. She felt that I was not suited for commercial school and that school was only for rich students to attend.

As if my abusive aunt was not enough, I had no peace with the neighbors in the yard. I was cursed at and called many names regularly, including queen, bitch, and whore. Even the adults joined in. What made matters worse was that I was allergic to mosquito bites. Whenever I scratched, the bumps turned into sores. Mama used to rub my skin with all sorts of funny smelling mixtures at bedtime, but nothing worked. She burned mosquito coils at night to keep away the mosquitoes. She even bought me a mosquito net to protect me while I slept. We had to close all the windows early before 7:00 p.m. so that the mosquitoes could not come into the house, but nothing ever worked, so my other nickname was "mangy."

No one would believe that I once played with these children without any problems. I stopped playing because I had to go to commercial school in the afternoons and on the weekends, which means I was engaged in other activities. Apart from that, I was also getting ahead of myself—too grown and too sophisticated to get involved in childish activities. I had better things to do with my time.

On one occasion, while I was bathing in the community bathroom, one of the young men came into the bathroom to rape me. I had to fight for my life, and I bit him. He ran out of the bathroom screaming. Even though he was unable to rape me, he taunted me every day from that point on. One of the young women, Charlotte, said that she was going to beat me up. My grandmother went to an attorney, Marcelle, who was also her nephew. He sent the girl a letter to cease and desist. She stopped her threats, but the others laughed whenever I passed by. All of that went on for several years.

That was a very difficult time for me during the beginning stages of my adolescent journey. I started questioning my identity and the very purpose of my existence. For example, my nickname was Buggie, but I wanted nothing to do with that name. I saw my birth certificate and that name was not there. I did not want to be called out of my name. Moreover, I was carrying the last name of a man that I did not know whom I believed did not want me to be a part of his life. I also thought that he had disowned me even though his name was on my birth certificate. Imagine my frustration when I asked my grandmother why I had to use his name and she said that she wanted me to know who my father was. That explanation was mindboggling—even to this day—because I still do not know who my father is.

When anyone in the yard called me Buggie, I promptly reminded them that my name was Ingrid. I just had to assert my own identity in the metamorphosis of my life. Some of the adults thought that it was cute to shorten my nickname to Buggs, but that irritated me even more.

Eventually, I stopped answering to those nicknames, which infuriated people because they thought that I was being rude and disrespectful. They complained to my grandmother. Mama promptly said to them, "Her name is Ingrid." That brought the name calling to an end. *Oh, what a relief!*

When I turned fourteen, my father stopped paying for child support through the courts since I was a bastard child. That was the law and therefore legal at that time. My mother came home and bought me a wristwatch with some of the money. She had allowed the money to accumulate in the courts for several months. She did not give Mama any of this money for me. As a matter of fact, she never gave Mama any money for me. Up to that point, my grandmother was struggling with me all by herself with only a little help from my Uncle Andy.

I wonder just what the British lawmakers were thinking when this child support law was enacted. A fourteen-year-old child cannot find full-time employment to support themself adequately—only menial jobs with low wages. The legal age for employment was eighteen. Of course, at age fourteen, a child could not acquire any employable skills.

My question is, *what makes a fourteen-year-old bastard child so different from a fourteen-year-old child born in wedlock?* We are all God's children. We did not ask to be born. We are the product of irresponsible people. Maybe if adults would be more mindful of their social and sexual activities, then bastardization would not be a source of inconvenience and embarrassment.

My father still had his legitimate fourteen-year-old child and older children living in his precious household. *Was I not worthy of the same support? What was I supposed to do without his support?* It was all mindboggling. It defied human logic that an illegitimate child would be treated differently because of the nature of their conception. On the other hand, a child born in wedlock was treated with the utmost care, love, and respect until age eighteen and even longer if the child was in school. That was indeed an unjust system.

I was ready to leave primary school by age fourteen. I finished early because I skipped two classes and passed all my exams. There was nowhere else for me to go and nothing else for me to do there. I did not want to become an assistant teacher at that time. I wanted to go to secondary school, but that would be a challenge for me. Private secondary school was even more expensive than commercial school.

But once again, I had a plan.

Since I already had advanced certificates, I could stop commercial school and save for high school instead. Also, I typed for my grandmother's friends and others who passed by and heard my loud typewriter in action. They recommended me to their friends because I did an excellent job for them. I used to read and correct their letters before I typed them. More money was coming in that way. Madam Thom also gave me some money for helping in her salon. I had some savings in the School Thrift Society and in my Milo/Ovaltine cans too. Thankfully, Uncle Andy was still making weekly contributions to Mama.

When I started high school, I had enough money to purchase my books, pay my tuition for the first semester, and purchase material for my school uniform and other supplies I needed. By that time, we had gotten another sewing machine, so I sewed a new school uniform. I made puffed sleeve shirts instead of the regular sleeves. When my mother saw my shirts, she said that they were going to take me out of the school because that was not the uniform. That did not happen, though. Everyone loved my modestly puffed sleeves.

When my aunt heard that I was heading for high school, she became even more enraged than before. She told all her friends that Mama was spoiling me and wasting her money and that I would be ungrateful. My grandmother did what she always did—she just rolled her eyes, hissed her teeth, and ignored my aunt.

The transition to high school was a challenge for me. It was very different from elementary school. I was shocked

My 14th Birthday. I am wearing my school
uniform that I made. I purchased my books,
briefcase, socks & shoes with the money I
earned.

to find out that there was a teacher for each subject. The workload was heavy because each teacher gave their own homework, and classes stuck to a regular schedule. Each student was given individual schedules of classes and were addressed differently. The boys had to be called by their last names, while the girls had to be called "Miss" and their last names, for example, I was called Miss Benjamin.

That school was ranked second-best in our region. I was placed in Form 4, which was the equivalent of a junior or Grade 11 here in the USA. There were six forms in some of our top high schools. Form 5 was equivalent to the senior year or Grade 12. The sixth form was equivalent to the first year of college in the USA. Very few students stayed long enough to enter the sixth form. Students who entered Form 6 took the *GCE Advanced Level*, another exam that came from England.

Most students left high school between Forms 4 and 5. This meant that they were between the ages of sixteen and eighteen. Some students pursued higher education in Teachers' College, University of Guyana, the Technical Institute, or Nursing School, or did apprenticeship training at a job site. Others just hung around until they were ready to make that crucial decision about their lives.

There were no high school graduations as those held in the USA. Graduations were only held at the university level. There was only an award ceremony at the end of the school year in college. The elementary and high schools had an awards ceremony at the end of each term. There were no proms or organized sports teams. As a matter of fact, physical education was optional, and that was held in the afternoons after school. I did not play an active role in sporting events. However, I supported my athletic friends in their endeavors which were held only one day during the school year when there were track and field competitions with other schools.

I was too cute to sweat, so physical activity was definitely not for me. I had no intention of running anywhere or jumping over anything. I attended Berbice Educational Institute, a predominately East Indian high

Off to High School. *I paid for the first term (semester) – 3 months tuition, bought my tie and accessories, books and uniform material with the money I saved. I made my own uniform including the shirts.*

school. Other races were in the minority. The students and teachers were awesome.

I made friends with four incredible young ladies. Phyllis and Donna lived on the Corentyne River and commuted daily. That made it difficult for us to associate after school. We talked after classes and when I got back to school after the lunch break. My other friends were Maureen and Ingrid. They lived in my hometown. We walked home every day after school. My grandmother gave them her seal of approval. According to her, they came from "good stock." This meant that their parents were outstanding citizens in the community. My grandmother pretty much chose my friends for me. She always said, "Show me your company and I'll tell you who you are."

Ingrid's father was in the military. He had a band for young people. Mama encouraged me to join it. Unfortunately, I had to purchase my own musical instrument and uniforms for the band. I also had to invest a lot of time in the afternoons to attend practice sessions. This would have been in direct conflict with my commercial school, and I was trying to complete my program at the end of that semester. After careful consideration, I decided not to join. It was not cost effective for me since I already had other monetary commitments. Moreover, I didn't think that being in a band would benefit me in the future. I had to remain focused on my goal.

My friends and I could not spend much time together outside of school. My grandmother had a tight leash on me. I was not allowed to go to the cinema or parties because of church rules. I could only go camping with adult supervision.

I thoroughly enjoyed my high school days since they gave me something to look forward to in the future. It gave me hope. All my friends had dreams, or, as my grandmother would have said, "ambition." Donna and Phyllis wanted to be teachers, Maureen wanted to be a nurse like her mother, and Ingrid wanted to be in banking with her older sister. I wanted to be a secretary or teacher— whichever one would take me out of the nigger yard faster!

As a teenager, I just couldn't identify with my living situation. It was embarrassing and very demeaning. I had to find a way out.

Meanwhile, I still had to study and do my homework in the wee hours of the mornings. My aunt was relentless and determined not to leave me alone because she did not want me to succeed. The courses in high school were relatively easy. It was just too many of them. If I were to become a success, I had to work harder and try to keep up. Physics was challenging to me, so I put more effort into it and studied harder.

The most amazing and incredible phenomenon happened to me in high school. It was a supernatural experience. One night, I went to bed very perplexed and worried that I was having a hard time with physics. In my dreams, I saw white handwriting on a blackboard. When I looked carefully, it was the steps to solve my physics problems. I heard no voice and saw no physical form of a body. I did not even see a face. I only saw the handwriting—the step-by-step illustrations and instructions—on the blackboard.

That continued throughout my high school years—not every night though. Whenever I was having a problem in math, physics, or chemistry, I went to bed and my tutoring session began. I was not afraid, but I never told anyone. Coupled with this experience, there were times when I slept that I would see a movie of my activities for the following day. The activities of the entire day would be revealed to me the night before. For example, whenever there was a pop quiz, I would see the subject and the questions, so I knew what to study when I awoke early in the morning. However, I never dreamed about a planned test. Once again, I never told a single soul because I did not want anyone to think I was crazy or describe me negatively. My mother already said that I would "run off" or go crazy if I did not stop studying.

During my tenure in high school there were many challenges. There were times when a teacher was absent. When this occurred, all of us would get into groups and review our work. In most cases the answers were at the back of the book, and this was helpful. I remember when our economics teacher quit and there was no replacement. We got together and each student studied parts of the text and taught the class during that period. We were not fortunate to have substitute teachers or anyone to supervise us whenever a teacher was absent. If we were going to be successful, then we had to make it happen for ourselves. There was no fooling around or horse play during our classes. We took the quizzes and tests from the back of the textbooks. We exchanged test papers and graded them. Talk about honesty—it seemed as though the students in my classes were all kindred souls, with an insatiable appetite for learning and well-defined goals for success.

Most of the students in my high school were on a mission. They came from very far away to attend school. Some students were up as early as three o'clock in the morning to catch a bus. The bus could only take them so far, and then they had to take a taxi or walk the rest of the way to school. Some students came from across the Berbice River from Rosignol or Blairmont, which meant that they had to wait for the Tourani, which was a very old and slow steamer boat. It was often off schedule and late. Some students took launches—small boats—to cross the Berbice River from Blairmont. Either way, students made great sacrifices to attend school. Most students took between one and three hours to get to school and just about the same time to get back home. Some students came from the Corentyne coast and had to travel for at least one to two hours by bus each way, depending on how far they lived.

As if the travel was not bad enough, all students, teachers, and residents in that area had to tread on a dirt road to get to their destination—school, work, or home. In my case, I only had to walk to school, which was just up the road less than a mile away. I even went home for lunch. May God help us when it rained. Wading through, skipping over, and navigating around large puddles was an art form to be mastered if you wanted to keep your uniform and shoes clean. Many of us wore goulashes and long boots on rainy days. Getting to school was a great and daunting transportation challenge, but it was worth it.

There were no cafeterias or lunchrooms in our school. Some of the students took their lunches and snacks with them, while others went home for lunch break, which was one and half hours long. Some students ate in the classrooms. Imagine the odor in there during lunch time. Lunches were all homemade—cooked food from scratch— no sandwiches, no store-bought food, and certainly, no fast foods. Fast foods were not available or even heard of at that time. A lot of families did not have gas or electric stoves. They cooked on kerosene oil stoves or firesides which was a very slow process. Imagine, students who lived far away had to get up early in the morning to cook food from scratch. Some parents got up early to cook also. In most cases, the food was placed in thermal flasks to keep warm.

My grandmother got up early in the morning to cook before she went to work. There were street vendors who sold snacks such as pholourie, bara, channa, and drinks such as mauby, swank or lemonade, and pine drink, as well as fruits at the side of the road. Those snacks were in glass cases or displayed on a tray. It's unbelievable that some of us made it through high school with perfect attendance, on time, and with excellent grades.

Meanwhile, my aunt, still full of hatred and jealousy, brought a fat "dougla" man—half African and half East Indian descent—into the house. She told my grandmother that he would help me with my studies. She showed him to the bedroom and told me to follow him. I did as I was told. When I got into the bedroom, he told me to bend over, and I did. He immediately pulled my underwear to the side and tried to insert his penis into my vagina.

When I felt the pain and pressure, I jumped and ran out of the room and told my grandmother. Mama immediately put him out. When I went to the front door, my aunt was sitting on the steps, peeping into the bedroom from a crease in the wall, to see what was happening. When she saw me, she became very adamant and asked, "whaa wrong with you?" as if I should have just leaned over to let that

Mrs. Pearl Stewart, my grandmother (Mama)

grown man rape me. When she came inside, a heated argument ensued with my grandmother. That was the first time I saw my grandmother angry. She even told my aunt to get out of her house. I wished that my aunt would have left us alone and moved on with her life, but she stayed and continued her evil ways.

When I thought about that incident, I often wondered about the condition of the human heart. *What would warrant an adult to bring a grown man home to have sex with a fifteen-year-old child?* Especially, when that child was her niece that she held as a baby and cared for as a young child. One would think her primary responsibility was to protect that child from all harm and danger. *Was it hate? Was it jealousy? Was it arrogance? Or just stupidity? Or did she want to destroy me so badly that she could not help herself?* I know that she did it on purpose to hurt me. I also wondered why Mama allowed me to go into the bedroom with that man. *Was she so overanxious for me to succeed in school?* I may never find the answers to these questions. I have since forgiven them. It is the right thing to do since I am now a Christian.

After that incident, I became very resentful towards my aunt. The next time she tried to punish me without cause, I picked up a machete and told her if she hit me, I would chop her up. I meant every word of it. That came from many years of stored-up anger and rage that I just had to let go. I even stopped speaking to her. Finally, she left me alone and never threatened me again nor imposed unnecessary chores and punishment on me.

However, she was never satisfied to see me at peace. Whenever she or any of her friends saw me talking to a boy, she would promptly inform Uncle Andy. He lived in McKenzie and had to travel all day to get to Mama's house. He believed every word that she said and would come home and hit me without asking me what the problem was. Somehow, I knew that he would hit me just before his departure to return to his home, so I ran to the cemetery and waited for him to leave.

One day when he came to mama's house, I asked him

Uncle Andy

why was he always hitting me when I did not do anything wrong. He told me that he did not want me to end up like my mother, making children without a future. He wanted me to get an education and become a powerful woman.

I said, "That's what I am doing. Please stop hitting me." I did not know he had such high hopes for me. That was the first time he expressed those positive sentiments.

Thankfully, the hitting stopped, but he was always suspicious and protective of me. He even protected me through college by making surprise visits on the pretense that he was bringing me money and food. Later, when he learned about my achievements, he was very proud of me. He gave me everything I wanted and would never listen to my evil aunt again. He would often tell his friends very proudly, "That's my niece!"

When my Mama got sick and could not go to work, Uncle Andy told her to stop working altogether. Without hesitation, she asked him what would happen to her Ingrid—me. He said that he would take care of me, and he put his money where his mouth was. Every week he sent a little more money to us. He paid for my trips, vacations, camps, exams, and just about everything else I needed. I never had to struggle for anything after that point.

Even though Uncle Andy was taking care of us, I continued to save my money as usual. Mama always encouraged me to "save for a rainy day." She also kept saying to me, "Mother has, father has, blessed is the child who has his own." When I was much younger, I did not understand what those sayings meant, but as I grew older and was faced with my own issues, the words became more meaningful and relevant to me.

Since Mama was no longer working, she stayed at home and made more scrap mats from my leftover sewing material. She also spent more time trying to get people to join her project known as the *Self-Help Housing Scheme Project*. She always said that when she left the "nigger yard" she wanted to go into her own home. She thought that was the easiest and most affordable path towards homeownership.

I only spent two years in high school. I took the national exam which came from England—the *General Certificate of Examination, Ordinary Level (GCE O Level)*. I passed with five subjects. The exam was equivalent to a high school diploma in the USA. I did not return to high school the following semester. Instead, I went to a tutor to get help preparing for a few more subjects at the GCE O Level. That was more economical than attending high school. I passed three more subjects, and my high school days were over. I was ready for the world.

Every week I saved some money in one of my two tin cans to pay my tuition for commercial school and later high school. I bought material to make my own clothes, bought my schoolbooks, paid for my exams, and took care of everything else I needed.

I got money when we sold chickens or eggs and I got money from my grandmother, Uncle Urban's wife Aunty Carmen, and Uncle Andy. I also got money when I typed documents for my grandmother's friends. Finally, I had saved money in the School Thrift Society.

Altogether, that was my savings plan and it worked like a charm.

Scrap Mat. Mama made scrap mats from my
left-over sewing materials. These mats could
be used on the floor, beds and chairs or
displayed on walls.

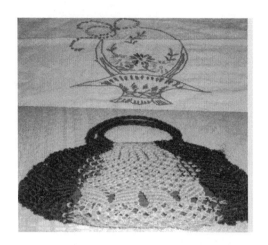

A hand towel (top). One of several hand towels I made in elementary school. One of several handbags I made (bottom).

WHAT WERE YOU THINKING?

by Melvina Jordan

How often do you stop to think about what it is you are thinking about? Close your eyes for a few seconds and ask yourself, "what am I thinking about?" and write it down on a piece of paper. Was it borrowed worry? An unfinished to-do list? Past disappointments or things you've lost? How about one of those "woulda, coulda, shouldas?" Was it selfish or sad? Giving or kind? Was it food? The beach? Was it fun? Whatever it was, write it down. Do this exercise anytime to gain perspective because thoughts guide us. They create feelings, mood swings, outlooks, attitudes, conversations, actions, stability, instability, and ultimately destinies.

Two dear friends of mine, that I've known for thirty years, husbands passed away even though we prayed for them. Then, my own husband of thirty-nine years became ill. Immediately, my thoughts—which seldom ask my permission to show up—began to create, in living color, pictures of gloom and doom. We cannot always control which thoughts arrive or when, but we can choose which ones we meditate on, so we must choose wisely.

Are you happy one minute but sad the next? James 1:1-8 says to ask God for wisdom, in faith, without wavering. "A double minded man is unstable in all his ways. Let not that man think that he shall receive anything of the Lord."

Learn to question wrong thinking. Joy has become my strength. Change can be quite positive. Instead of thinking about the worst-case scenarios, I choose to think of the best. I think we can finally enjoy those brand-new rocking chairs we bought years ago, but never used, to sit outside and sip our coffee in the front yard. I think about how much we enjoy those one-day trips we started to take with our Griswell Senior Center friends like that prime rib brunch river boat cruise with a live band. I think about how we attend church together again and visit our gym's indoor pool, hot tub, and sauna more now. I think about the wisdom of our two awesome sons and the cuteness of our one and three-year-old grandsons we now visit some Sundays. We seldom made time for them before, due to our demanding careers. I think about things that are good, true, honest, just and pure, and of good report. I think about these things. I have chosen to think on gratitude verses "what ifs."

None of us have control over how or where we started, but we have huge control over how and where we end up. I have learned that my outcome is mostly in my own hands. That outlook is so important even if you are not exactly where you want or planned to be. It all starts with what we are thinking about, what we choose to meditate on, act on, believe in, and then set out to create with follow through.

Most career criminals meditate on ways to commit crime. They mentally prepare. When I was obese, my thoughts were focused on the deliciousness of my next meal long before I finished what I was currently eating. What do you think about often? We can choose what we meditate on. This is not easy, and it requires much practice. I keep at it. I keep my Bible and a good novel near my bed. I keep wholesome television shows recorded to watch when I feel anxious.

Be mindful of what goes into your thinking—garbage in, garbage out as the saying goes. Again, choose wisely. Make daily decisions to dwell on thoughts of good, of peace, and of what you have instead of what you do not. Dwell on thoughts that encourage you. Which of us by being worried can add value or a single hour to our lives? Quite the opposite. Dwell on thoughts that guide you in the directions you want to go. Each day has the possibility of being a blessing if you let it. Your future can be as good as or better than your past. Do not let the only way to stop wrong thinking be alcohol, illegal drugs, handcuffs, or prescription medication—all of these put you in a kneeling position. Take the handcuffs off your optimism! Be self-correcting, proactive, and considerate in your thinking. Excellent mental health is a process—a journey—and a most precious gift to be envied. Place yourself in a position of hopefulness. When you change your thinking, you can change your life.

See YOU at the beach!

Mrs. Melvina "Tea" Jordan, Retired Police Sergeant (State of Georgia), Certified Anger Management Specialist II, Domestic/Family Violence-MRT Senior Court Facilitator, Prison/Nursing Home Ministry

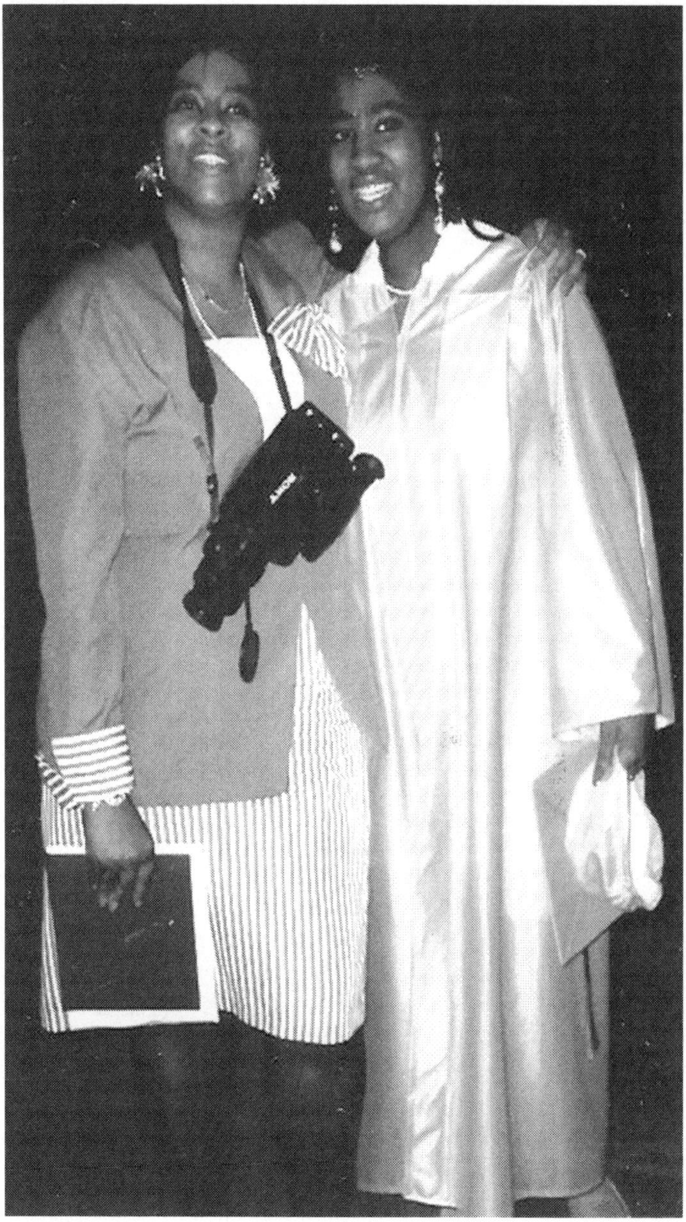

I love you, Mom.

CAUSE AND EFFECT

by Peggy Sue Bellot

In this chapter, there will be no excuses—just facts. However, there will be causes and effects teamed with apologies. I will give explanations for some of the hardships that affected you in our lives. You will always have my most sincere apologies. I will try to give you some insight with honesty and truth of the experiences of single parenting. Come now, the causes and effects...

To my dear children:

The year was 1972. I was seventeen years old when I met your father. By the time I turned eighteen, we were steady dates. Your dad was twenty-three years old and a tall, lean, handsome man. I was so pleased with him.

Up until l met your dad, I lived my life for the most part as a loner. My mother worked at the Fort Street Post Office in Detroit, Michigan. My dad worked at Ford Motor Company just outside of Detroit. My older sister and brother were straight A students. They lived in their own worlds and had their own separate interests. My mother and my brother attended Cass Technical High School which, at that time, was a school that was strictly for students with high grade point averages.

Growing up as a young girl, I spent a lot of time doing homework, trying to keep up with my older brother and sister—both academic geniuses. By the time I turned thirteen, I inherited a baby brother that I babysat. Back in the day, the older children looked after the younger children. Of course, my baby brother was a straight A student as well.

As a child I always felt like an outsider and loner; however, as I grew older and communicated with my siblings, we all discovered that each of us felt that way. Maybe we felt like that because we each pursued different interests. God only knows how much and how deeply I love my sister and brothers.

Growing up, I never heard my mom or dad tell me they loved me. I never ever remember my mom or dad hugging me after the age of five years old. I can remember my mom hugging me once and I had to be about two years old. I woke up one morning and the sun was shining through my bedroom window onto my old-fashioned wallpaper that had little red designs. I jumped out of bed and ran through the hallway and down the stairs. I jumped from the last two steps and ran into the den. I surprised my mother and she smiled and swept me up into her arms. She started singing to me the song, *oh where, oh where has my little dog gone*. She sang that song all the way through to the end while I was in her arms. When she finished, a dog started barking on our back porch. We both looked surprised and started laughing.

Before I started school, I would be at home with just my mom. My dad would come home around two in the afternoon from work every day. I could hear his car from anywhere in our house. When daddy pulled up, I would run out the house down the steps and up to his car. Daddy would pick me up high into the air and give me a kiss attack. I had pancake cheeks, but after he gave me a kiss attack, I could feel my face spasm. My spasms, after he kissed me, were because of his five o'clock stubble. Daddy shaved very often, so I could never figure out that stubble on his face.

Growing up I just did not have human relationship skills. I felt best when I was by myself. I was always being picked on. People just did not like me. I was called a "yellow scab" even though I was brown skinned. I was told that I was spit on in my crib when I was a baby. People that I heard of but did not know always wanted to fight me. I was told that some people would say *hello* or *hi* to me and I would not speak. Truthfully, I just did not see or hear them. I believe that I had a one-track mind. Couple that with shyness and an inability to communicate with others and it was a recipe for disaster. Sometimes people interpreted this as being "uppity." In reality, I was the last person on earth to be uppity—I loved people.

I did have a few close friends, but they were my total opposites. They were outgoing and saw in me something they seemed to appreciate. I was happy to be around anyone that would talk to me and not call me names, criticize me, or want to beat me up.

A few of the friends I thank God for are Wanda Browning, Gwendolyn Phillips, Iris Wilson, Cherise Beasley, Sylvia Godfrey, Sharon Ponder, and Josie Fox.

Because there were no I-love-you's or hugs in my house, I did not place a value on hugs or expressing love. Somehow, I always knew that my mother, father, sister, and brothers loved me in their hearts. They too did not know how to verbalize love or physically show it. What's interesting is that, in contrast, my parents could reach our very souls with a belt to the behind or legs when we got out of line. Discipline was always administered, promptly when we did wrong, and it worked well for me. I decided that I would get as few whippings as possible especially after a cherry tree branch was introduced into the mix.

To remedy my non communicative life at home, I became active in as many entities as I could. I joined the Girl Scouts, the summer drama club, the softball team, the science club, the math club, and I took after school swim classes. I became a Sunday school teacher, a Girl Scouts leader, and a member of the Pan-African Group. I did modern dance, performing at times, and I also belonged to my junior high school orchestra

Even after all the extracurricular activities, my shyness remained, and my communication and people skills were bleak. I guess I could only focus on one thing at a time. My parents hardly ever had time to talk to me about life or even about "the birds and the bees." However, Daddy did teach me one thing that I will always remember, "when you have obstacles, trouble, and problems in life, do the best to fix them and to hell with that which you cannot fix."

My parents were more concerned with us doing our homework and getting good grades in school than showing us love. Honestly, I think this was just their generation and they showed us love the best way they knew how. Actually, they showed love every day because every day they provided us with a roof over our heads, food, clothing, and the necessary "daily bread."

Fast forward from childhood—I met my first husband when I was seventeen years old. By the time I was eighteen, we were kind of dating, and he was my only date until I turned nineteen. We got married when I was nineteen and he was twenty-five years old. I left the only home I had ever known and went directly from my parents' house to my husband's. He fathered my first two kids.

My husband could not understand why I was so ignorant about the outside world—add that to my shyness and poor communication skills and it made me look even worse. I married a man who had been on his own for quite a few years. He had fought in the Vietnam War and had a steady job. Our match was more of a mismatch than anything.

My marriage got to the point where whenever he got angry, he would just reach out and proceed to hit, push, knock, slap, or outright fight me. Every time he put his hands on me to hurt me, I would call my father or brother. They would come and take me to my mother's or father's house where I would be safe. I would stay with either parent until I was convinced by my husband that he would never hurt me again—we did this dance too often. I always ended up back with my husband until the next big fight.

One day my husband beat me badly. When I came to, I was lying under a bedroom window with pain running through my head. When he first hit me, I recall I was at the bedroom door. Inside the bedroom, there was a queen size bed between the door and the window I woke up under. To this day, the only thing I can remember is him cursing me and his angry ugly face while he raised his fist. Actually, he was handsome, but when he was angry, he was ugly. My face was badly bruised, and my eye was black and blue and badly swollen. I remember after that beating, he did not want me to leave the house as that would embarrass him, and people would know the truth about him.

After the last and most horrible incident, I decided that I would call the police any and every time he beat or hit me—he mostly would hit me. I was getting close to my breaking point. I would not call Daddy or my brother anymore—just the police.

The incident that brought me back to my senses was the day when I was seven months pregnant, and my husband decided that he would beat me. He got in a few good licks before I managed to call the police. The police came and escorted me out of the house. He came out of the house after me. The police flashed their lights on him. All our neighbors were outside watching. The police officers started telling him that he was wrong to fight a pregnant, defenseless woman, and how evil he was for doing so. They also told him that he better not ever again put his hands on me if he knew what was good for him. Today, I am blessed to say my first husband grew up too. He now serves the Lord and always lends a helping hand to whoever needs it.

My husband crossed the line when he beat me while I was pregnant. I called my daddy one more time, and this was the last time. This also was the last time my daddy came over to rescue me, but he did not actually rescue me. Daddy assured me that he loved me, and I was always welcome in his house but only under the following conditions.

Daddy told me in simple terms "Peggy, you can stay with your husband and let him beat you until you die, or you could leave him and leave him for good."

I took the latter choice and decided that day that I would leave my evil husband for good.

I planned for a whole year by getting rid of stuff and hiding money—what little I could get. I had just enough money for Greyhound tickets with $15 left over for all the necessities. During that year, I was very kind to my husband. If he called me a bitch or cursed at me, I would apologize to him. I would even tell him I would be his bitch. If he hit me, I would just take it. I cooked, cleaned, and did all my wifely duties with a smile on my face and with kindness. I did everything I could to make his life as pleasant as I could.

The day finally came when I boarded that Greyhound bus for California. My adopted sister knew about the violence and had invited me to bring my kids and move in with her. I had one seven-month-old baby and a two-year-old daughter. I had my diaper bag, an overnight bag, and my two babies with me. That trip was hard as hell.

After I left home and my husband behind, I began my life as a single, ignorant parent trying to raise two small kids. First of all, I would like to apologize to my daughter and sons for all the many errors I made and the suffering they endured because of my life, which was extremely hard.

I made some mistakes in my life and my mistakes rained down on my kids and gave them some bad experiences in life. I wish I could go back and clean up all the mistakes I made in raising them. Unfortunately, I cannot.

I pray my kids forgive me. I hurt deep in my soul and heart for all the hardships they went through. I have always prayed to God for help in trying to live with my mistakes and the pain my life caused others. Not too long ago I got an answer to my prayers. God forgave me. *THANK YOU, JESUS.* I have even learned to forgive myself.

If anything, please do not let past hurts and pains and experiences affect your life. Go forward and pursue your dreams. Even if I were never to be forgiven by my children, I pray they will go forward and do their best to live the best life they can.

Look up, always. We serve an amazing God. Children, I know that you have spirit and soul. I have seen how you have forged ahead, and you are awesome in your own spirit.

My dear children, this is just the beginning of our story.

Made in the USA
Columbia, SC
09 November 2022

70694369R00145